ECONOMIC AID TO
UNDERDEVELOPED COUNTRIES

ECONOMIC AID
TO UNDERDEVELOPED
COUNTRIES

FREDERIC BENHAM

Henry Price Professor of International Economics
at the Royal Institute of International Affairs

Issued under the auspices of the
Royal Institute of International Affairs

OXFORD UNIVERSITY PRESS
LONDON NEW YORK TORONTO

Oxford University Press, Amen House, London E.C.4

GLASGOW NEW YORK TORONTO MELBOURNE WELLINGTON
BOMBAY CALCUTTA MADRAS KARACHI LAHORE DACCA
CAPE TOWN SALISBURY NAIROBI IBADAN ACCRA
KUALA LUMPUR HONG KONG

PRINTED IN GREAT BRITAIN

CONTENTS

CHAPTER I

THE UNDERDEVELOPED COUNTRIES

INTRODUCTION

THERE is a widespread belief that more economic aid should be provided for underdeveloped countries. Although this view is not shared by all, it has been expressed by many prominent people in the chief industrial countries. One consequence is that a Development Assistance Group of nine nations (Belgium, Canada, France, Germany, Italy, Portugal, Japan, the United Kingdom, and the United States) was set up early in 1960 to study the problem of co-ordinating bilateral and multilateral aid programmes. Another consequence is that the International Development Association was established in September 1960, for the purpose of making loans on easy terms to low-income countries. It is affiliated to the World Bank and has a planned capital of $1,000 million.

The main purpose of this book is to discuss a number of questions which arise in connexion with economic aid. The next chapter sets out the present position: how much economic aid is provided, in what forms and through what channels, and who are the chief contributors and recipients. Chapter III discusses the view that underdeveloped countries need trade rather than aid. Chapter IV considers the part played by the flow of private capital. The last chapter considers various arguments for and against providing economic aid and draws some conclusions, suggesting that the amount provided should be substantially increased and made more effective.

First, however, it seems necessary to say something about the underdeveloped countries and their problems, in order to show why they need some form of economic assistance. As thousands of books and articles have already been written on this subject, I shall keep my remarks as brief as possible.

DEVELOPED AND UNDERDEVELOPED COUNTRIES

The more advanced, or industrial, countries are usually taken to be the United States and Canada; the United Kingdom and the countries of Western Europe; Australia and New Zealand; and the Soviet Union and Japan. Most other countries, especially the poorer countries of Asia, Africa, and Latin America, are classed as less developed, or underdeveloped.

This distinction is not based on the scope for further development; if it were, then Canada, for example, with her vast area, large and varied natural resources, and small population, would be considered underdeveloped. It is based mainly on the size of real income per head and partly on the extent of industrialization. The former group have much higher real incomes than most of the latter. However the distinction is to some extent arbitrary. Some countries, for example Argentina and the Union of South Africa, are in an intermediate position, while a number are divided regionally, as Italy is divided into the industrial north and the poor and agricultural south. Some countries in the former group, such as New Zealand, Denmark, and even Australia, are not very industrialized and export mainly agricultural products (although only a minority of their workers are engaged in agriculture); but they have high incomes. The Soviet Union and Japan are included because they are industrialized, although they have lower real incomes per head than some of the so-called underdeveloped countries.[1]

The size of national income per head of population is the most comprehensive single measure of the wealth or poverty of a country. It shows extremely wide differences. For example, the present figure for India is about £25 a year as compared with over £350 in this country and twice as much in the United States.

No doubt such figures exaggerate the differences quite considerably. In the poorer countries most families perform services for themselves in the home which are to some extent performed for money payments in industrial countries; domestic service, preparing and cooking food, baking, washing clothes, and dressmaking are leading examples. Such services therefore do not enter into their national-income figures, whereas in industrial countries they do. Again, many poor countries consist largely of more or less self-sufficient village communities, which do not have to pay transport costs for people going to work or for commodities imported from elsewhere; whereas such costs of transport and distribution play a large part in the national incomes of the more developed countries. Again, in hot countries there is obviously less need for fuel, warm clothing, and solidly built houses, and experts think that the amount of food needed is considerably smaller than in colder climates.

For these and other reasons, the conversion of national incomes per head into a common currency at current exchange rates often makes the differences seem greater than they really are. The exchange equivalent of a U.S. dollar may buy much more, especially more labour services, in countries where incomes are low than in the United States.

[1] On its official figures the Soviet Union may claim to be a high-income country, but her standards of living are still quite low.

Nor is income per head the sole criterion. In the poorer countries many workers enjoy more leisure (although this may be due to lack of employment opportunities, or debilitating diseases or malnutrition, rather than deliberate choice) than in the more advanced countries. Japan has a lower income per head than, for example, the Federation of Malaya, but she enjoys higher and more widespread levels of education, better standards of housing, and more varied employment opportunities. Venezuela has the highest average income per head in Latin America, but, at least until recently, this was very unevenly distributed, and the mass of the people were poverty-stricken peasants.

However, even after we take all such factors into account, we cannot escape the conclusion that there are quite large differences between standards of living in the more advanced countries and in most of the others. The amount of food consumed in the former is over 3,000 calories per person per day. In the underdeveloped countries it is considerably less. In the poorest, it is only about 2,000, and consists largely of starchy foods such as yams, cassava, and cheap grains; it includes little protein in the form of meat or fish, and little milk or other dairy products. Standards of clothing and housing are also low. The amount of cloth consumed is 10 to 15 yards or less per person per year, as compared with several times that amount in the wealthier countries; and their houses are mostly miserable shacks of wood or mud and wattle. As to health, there are far fewer doctors and nurses per million of population than in the more advanced countries; death-rates are considerably higher, especially for babies and young children; and in some of these countries diseases such as malaria and tuberculosis are still widespread. Similarly with education: on the average, only half the children in underdeveloped countries get any kind of schooling at all; often the primary course lasts only four or five years, and attendances of those enrolled are poor; and the great majority of adults are illiterate.

DIFFERENCES AMONG UNDERDEVELOPED COUNTRIES

I have stressed the contrast between the richer countries and the poor countries. But the so-called underdeveloped countries (including China)[2] contain over two-thirds of the population of the world; they show such diversity in levels of income per head, extent of industrialization, standards of health and education, and so forth, that it is difficult to make generalizations which apply to them all.

The chief oil-exporting countries form a special category. In my view, their present revenues from oil are so large that they need little or no external aid.[3] This applies to Venezuela, several Middle East countries (notably Iran, Iraq, Kuwait, and Saudi Arabia), and Brunei (but possibly not to Trinidad and certainly not to Indonesia).

Three of the ways in which the various underdeveloped countries differ from one another are especially significant. They are: the degree to which they are overpopulated or underpopulated, the extent to which they specialize on exports, and the extent to which their economies are controlled by their governments.

[2] By China I mean Communist China, not Taiwan (Formosa).

[3] Venezuela has been receiving the equivalent of over £250 million a year and the four Middle East countries that of over £400 million a year between them as oil revenue. Libya (with oil reserves said to be as large as those of Kuwait and a population of less than 2 million) may soon be in that category, but not Algeria.

It need hardly be said that most of the oil-exporting countries would not agree with this view, especially Iran and Iraq. Iraq has an ambitious development programme and is at present receiving appreciable economic aid from both Communist and non-Communist sources. Even Venezuela now claims that she has seriously overspent and needs substantial economic aid.

Overpopulation and Underpopulation

Some countries are heavily overpopulated. Most of them are predominantly agricultural. The average size of family farm is very small, much too small to provide an adequate livelihood. Their output per worker would be increased, and their standards of living thereby raised, if their numbers could be substantially reduced as time goes on. Leading examples are India, China, Java (but not the rest of Indonesia), and some of the Caribbean islands. Japan also is in this category, but Japan is usually regarded as a developed country, which should and does provide, rather than receive, external aid.

On the other hand, some countries are relatively under-populated. They still have a good deal of undeveloped culti-vable land. The growth of their populations would tend to raise output per head by making possible more speciali-zation and more large-scale production, opening-up their countries, and providing more traffic for their existing trans-port facilities and larger sales for their existing factories, power stations, and so forth. A considerable part of Latin America and of Africa, and some countries (for example, Burma) in Asia are in this category.

The great hardship of heavy overpopulation is illustrated by India. The present population of India is about 400 million. This includes over 10 million landless labourers and their families and about 20 million engaged in small-scale industry and handicrafts, such as hand-loom weaving. The total number employed in factories is only 3 million. The great majority of workers are engaged in agriculture. Most of the holdings are less than 5 acres and many less than one. As the Planning Commission points out, 'the scope for increasing the area under cultivation is extremely limited'. Even if the irrigated area could be nearly doubled (from 67 million acres in 1956 to 120 million), this would eventually raise output by only 17 per cent.[4]

India is already heavily overpopulated. But if death-rates fall, as malaria and other diseases are stamped out, towards the levels already achieved by countries such as Ceylon, and birth-rates remain high, population will double in the next thirty years.[5]

No doubt efforts to raise output per worker in agriculture (for example, by fostering the 'Japanese method' of rice cultivation) will show some results. No doubt progress with industrialization will continue, especially with the steel industry, for which India has large reserves of rich iron ore and also coking coal. New exports (to pay for food imports) may be developed, but 'as far as 95% of the exports from India are concerned, there is little likelihood of any marked increase even over the next two decades'.[6]

Whether increased output in agriculture, manufacturing, and other fields will be sufficient to achieve the aims of Indian planners, and to give a continuous improvement in standards of living—for some 800 million people by 1990— is very doubtful. What seems clear is that a reduction in birth-rates, and the sooner the better, would greatly improve India's economic prospects.

The Extent of Specialization on Exports

The proportion of its output which a country exports varies considerably from one country to another, from nearly 100 per cent. for Kuwait to about 5 per cent. for India.

[4] For these and other data, see Ansley J. Coale and Edgar M. Hoover, *Population Growth and Economic Development in Low-Income Countries; A Case Study of India's Prospects* (Princeton University Press, 1958).

[5] The Indian Planning Commission considers that the present population may be well over 400 million and may be 480 million in 1966.

[6] S. H. Patel, 'Export Prospects and Economic Growth: India' *Economic Journal*, Sept. 1959.

On the whole, it is the smaller countries which rely most on exports (although there are notable exceptions, such as Canada and Australia). This is because a large country is likely to have a wide range of climates, soils, and other natural resources; what would be international trade if each State or province were a separate country becomes internal trade when they are all unified, or federated, under one national Government.

Many underdeveloped countries have natural advantages of climate or soil which enable them to specialize on exporting certain agricultural products. Thus, to give only a few leading examples, the main export of the Federation of Malaya and Indonesia is rubber; of Egypt, cotton; of Cuba, sugar; of Brazil and Colombia, coffee; of Ceylon, tea; of Ghana, cocoa; of the Philippines, copra. Some countries export mainly minerals. The leading examples are those exporting oil, but a few others rely largely on exports of other minerals, as Chile does on copper. It is exceptional for an underdeveloped country to export mainly manufactures, but Hong Kong, which has cheap and efficient labour, exports cotton textiles and other manufactures to the value of over £50 million a year.

It is true that a country which derives a substantial part of its income, as many underdeveloped countries do, from its export earnings from one or two primary products may suffer a severe setback if there is a marked fall in their prices. This point is discussed in Chapter III. Nevertheless international trade enables such a country to import goods which it could not produce for itself (such as fuel) or which it could not produce so cheaply. The great drawback of being deprived of export markets, and compelled to become self-sufficient, was made very plain to those Asian countries which were occupied by the Japanese during the Second World War.

China and India have such large populations that they are almost bound to grow most of their own food; they export only about 5 per cent. of their total output. Some countries which were once large exporters of food are now exporting less owing to their increased populations and the growing proportion living in towns. Argentina is a leading example.

A number of underdeveloped countries have been aiming at greater self-sufficiency, producing for themselves goods formerly imported, especially manufactures of consumer goods (such as cotton textiles) and primary products, such as cereals and sugar. Nevertheless the volume of world trade has continued to expand. It is now about double what it was in 1938 and 50 per cent. greater than in 1950.

The Extent of State Control

Among non-Communist underdeveloped countries most Governments engage in much the same kinds of economic activities. In addition to providing for general administration, social services, defence, roads, and other purposes undertaken by all Governments, they own and operate public utilities, such as rail transport and electric power; they initiate, finance, and carry out any large-scale developments, such as irrigation projects, which may be undertaken to expand agricultural output; and a growing number of them have set up, or are planning to set up, industrial establishments such as steel mills, oil refineries, and chemical and fertilizer plants.

The arguments for public, rather than private, enterprise in such fields are discussed in Chapter IV. The amounts spent, relatively to needs, on various purposes, such as education, vary considerably from one country to another, depending mainly on how much each country can afford. Some Governments, for example that of Turkey, own a considerable number of factories, and others (for example, those of the poorer territories of Africa and the smaller Latin American republics) hardly any. Again, some Governments, for example that of India, exercise more control than others over such matters as prices (especially the retail prices of basic foodstuffs), international trade, and the operations of private enterprises. On the whole, however, the resemblances between the kinds of things that such Governments do are greater than the differences. The great contrast is, of course, between the Communist countries and the others. The economies of the former are completely planned and controlled by the state, while the latter retain the institutions (modified to a greater or less extent by governmental activities and legislation) of private property, freedom of enterprise, and freedom of choice by consumers.

China is by far the most important of those Communist countries which are still underdeveloped. She has attracted much attention by her rapid progress towards industrialization and by her expansion of output, especially in heavy industries, during recent years. Her standards of living are still very low, and the statistics published (but subsequently revised heavily downwards) by her Government purporting to measure her rapid economic growth, especially during the 'great leap forward' of 1958, were much exaggerated. Nevertheless there is no doubt that substantial economic progress has been achieved.[7]

This has raised the question of whether other underdeveloped countries, especially in Asia, should not follow the example of China and adopt some form of Communism

[7] For these and other data on China, see T. J. Hughes and D. E. T. Luard, *The Economic Development of Communist China 1949–58* (London, OUP for RIIA, 1959). Choh-ming Li, 'Economic Development', *The China Quarterly*, no. 1, Jan.-Mar. 1960, p. 37, estimates the rate of growth of net domestic (material) product during 1953–7 as 6 to 7 per cent. a year, against a population growth of 2·2 per cent. a year.

in order to speed up their development. India, which in a number of ways resembles China, seems to have made considerably less progress during recent years. That is one reason why the United States and other Western countries have recently provided, and are proposing to offer, more economic aid to India. They would like to show that India, a democratic country which maintains personal freedoms, can do as well as China (with some assistance from the Soviet Union) has done under Communism.

Complete state control enables a Government to enforce a high level of saving and investment. In a poor country, this usually means depressing still further standards of living which are already low. Labour, materials, and other resources are diverted from producing food and other goods for current consumption, and employed instead in constructing means of production such as power stations, railways, roads, factories, and irrigation projects. Such an increase of capital assets is necessary to make possible a growing expansion of output in the future, but for the time being it involves hardship and sacrifice.

In China, the Government obtains resources for investment in various ways. It imposes heavy taxation. It charges high prices, thus making substantial 'profits', on a number of goods produced by government factories. It compels workers and others to subscribe to issues of government bonds. It compels farmers producing more than sufficient for their own requirements (or collective farms) to sell stated amounts of their produce to the Government at low prices.

Similar methods may be used in non-Communist countries. For example, during the post-war period, the State Agricultural Marketing Board in Burma has provided the Government with a substantial revenue by paying about half the equivalent export price for rice (paddy) which the growers were compelled to sell to it. In general, however, people are not prepared to accept as much hardship and sacrifice, in order to speed up development, as they can be forced to accept in a Communist country such as China. The budgets of most non-Communist underdeveloped countries amount to only 10 to 15 per cent., or less, of the national income, as against 30 per cent. in China. The total amount of investment is only 10 per cent. or less of the national income in most of such countries, as against over 20 per cent. in China. Under a system of parliamentary democracy, a Government which taxes people more heavily than they consider proper, or which interferes too much with their personal freedom, is likely to be turned out at the next election. Even a dictatorship which makes itself unpopular by such measures may well be overthrown by force. A Communist dictatorship cannot go too far, as witness the changes in policy (towards a larger output of consumer goods) which have taken place from time to time in Communist countries. But it can go a long way if it can persuade people that Communism will give them, eventually, better standards of living; and either a Communist or any other dictatorship can go a long way if those in power are well protected against revolt or disobedience by the apparatus of a police state.

On the question of the economic progress made by China (after discounting exaggerated claims) some comments may be offered. It must be remembered that the Communist régime was welcomed by most of the Chinese people (other than the wealthier property-owners, most of whom nevertheless pretended to welcome it) because it contrasted very favourably with the former Government, which was generally considered corrupt, and ineffective in promoting economic stability and growth. Moreover the years under Communism (that is, since 1949) were the first period for forty years during which China has been, at home, free from wars and civil disturbances. It must also be remembered that some assistance (which, however, had to be paid for as time went on) was given by the Soviet Union, especially in setting up industrial establishments and providing technicians.

A further point is that for one reason or another the Chinese, in my view, seem to be more hard-working and more able to learn and practise improved methods than the people of most underdeveloped countries.

Relatively faster economic progress in China than in most Asian and other underdeveloped countries during recent years may be due to these factors rather than to the alleged superiority of Communism as an economic system.

POPULATION TRENDS

Most underdeveloped countries are experiencing what has been called a 'population explosion'. Since the war their rate of natural increase has shot upwards. In many of them it now approaches or exceeds $2\frac{1}{2}$ per cent. a year, and in a few it is over 3 per cent. a year. This compares with 0·7 per cent. for Europe (0·4 per cent. for the United Kingdom) and 1·8 per cent. for the United States.[8]

This has come about by a marked fall in death-rates, while birth-rates have remained very high, in many countries approaching or exceeding 40 per 1,000. Death-rates have fallen owing to improvements in health services, including new drugs, and especially to successful campaigns against various endemic diseases, in which the World Health Organization has taken a leading part. An outstanding example is Ceylon, where malaria was virtually wiped out just after the war. Crude death-rates fell from 20·3 per 1,000 in 1946 to

[8] These are 1953–7 rates (1950–7 for Europe) given in the U.N. *Demographic Year Book 1958*, Tables 1 and 2.

14·3 in 1947 and are now about 10, but birth-rates have remained somewhat higher than the pre-war level of 35 to 36 per 1,000.

The work of WHO continues. In its last (1958) annual report, it points out that it is engaged in a world-wide malaria-eradication programme, and in campaigns against other diseases in various countries. In its introduction to this report, it points out that many of the original handicaps remain unchanged; in particular, 'the shortage of trained and even semi-trained personnel is still very acute, and, in many places, downright critical', while 'the state of environmental sanitation remains unsatisfactory'.

It seems probable that, as time goes on, increased expenditure on public health will gradually overcome these handicaps, and that the continued efforts of the WHO and of Governments will lead to further falls in death-rates, especially in countries where they are still relatively high. Whether any marked fall in birth-rates will take place is much more doubtful. It may come about through propaganda, the discovery of efficient and cheap oral contraceptives, the more widespread legalization of abortion (in Japan there are nearly two abortions for every live birth), and growing urbanization; but at present there are few signs of any downward trends.

Population of Underdeveloped Countries
(millions)

	1958	1980	% Increase
Asia	1,580	2,470	56
Africa	227	333	47
Latin America	197	349	77
Total	2,004	3,152	57

Source: FAO, *The State of Food and Agriculture 1959* (Rome, 1959), p. 134.

The most likely prospect, therefore, is that the populations of underdeveloped countries will continue to grow faster than those of the more advanced countries. While any population forecast is liable to considerable error it seems probable that the underdeveloped countries, which at present have two-thirds, more or less (depending on how many 'intermediate' countries such as Argentina are included), of a world population of nearly 3 milliard, will by 1980 have over three-quarters of a world population somewhat exceeding 4 milliard.

A rapidly growing population means a high proportion of children. In most countries of Asia, Africa, and Latin America, the proportion of children under 15 years of age is about 40 per cent. of the total, as compared with some 25 per cent. in Western Europe and North America. In a relatively underpopulated country the growth of numbers may eventually increase output per head, although in a relatively overpopulated country it will tend to do the opposite; but in any country a high proportion of dependent children is for the time being a drain on its resources. They have to be provided with food and other requirements, including, if possible, education, and eventually with employment opportunities. Capital, and current output, which would otherwise raise standards of living, have to be used instead for the growing number of children.

It would seem, therefore, that the problems of the underdeveloped countries are likely to become quantitatively more serious owing to the rapid growth of their populations.

SOME CONTROVERSIES ABOUT ECONOMIC GROWTH

The factors affecting economic growth are very numerous. Moreover, conditions vary so much among countries that the most suitable measures and priorities for each particular country must be studied on the spot in the light of all relevant local circumstances. Some general issues, however, may be briefly discussed. I shall consider some controversial issues to which an aid-giving country or organization might well attach considerable weight if its purpose is to stimulate and assist economic growth in the recipient country. It is true that the latter is fully entitled to say: 'We are an independent country; we shall decide entirely for ourselves what course we consider best, and we shall accept no aid with any kinds of strings attached to it.' But the former is equally entitled to say: 'We believe that it is imperative, entirely in your own interests, to give such-and-such measures priority; we believe that such-and-such policies would be detrimental, not helpful, to your economic growth; and unless you do what we think best for you, we shall not provide any aid.' Obviously these two extreme attitudes may often be modified by a compromise, given sufficient tact, patience, and understanding on both sides.

A major controversy concerns the priority which underdeveloped countries should give to industrialization. Most of the wealthy countries are highly industrialized, so that the short cut to greater wealth for countries which are mainly agricultural may seem to be the rapid establishment of manufacturing industries. This is the advice given by the Soviet Union; and any contrary views expressed by Western countries tend to be attributed to their self-interest, for they are exporters of manufactures.

Nevertheless there are strong arguments in favour of what is sometimes called 'balanced growth'. To begin with, the basic material need of mankind is food; the lower a person's income the greater is the proportion of it which he spends on food. Leaving aside international trade, if the labour of six or seven or eight families is needed to provide enough food for ten families, then 60 or 70 or 80 per cent. of the population must be engaged in agriculture, in producing food. In most underdeveloped countries, this is in fact the position; 60 or 70 or 80 per cent. of their workers are engaged in producing food, and even so their diets are not adequate for health and efficiency either in quantity or quality. In the richer countries of the world, the percentage of the population in agriculture is much lower and the output per worker in agriculture is far higher, often ten times or more higher.

The industrial revolutions of the more advanced countries, including Japan, were long cumulative processes, involving improvements in the technique of agriculture, expansion of means of transport, and better education and training of workers, as well as technical advances in manufacturing processes. History need not repeat itself. The underdeveloped countries can borrow the most advanced technical methods from the West (in so far as they are suitable; some are too capital-intensive for countries where labour is plentiful and capital scarce) instead of slowly discovering them for themselves, and they can draw on the capital as well as on the technical knowledge and expert assistance of the more advanced countries. They may therefore be able to develop more rapidly than the latter did.

Nevertheless it seems clear that one of their primary aims should be a progressive increase in their output per worker in agriculture. This would provide them with more food. It would set free workers to move (after training) into manufacturing and other non-agricultural occupations. At the same time, it would expand their home markets for local manufactures. Since most of their workers are at present engaged in agriculture, it is the purchasing-power which they get from sales of their produce, over and above the amounts needed for their own consumption, which provides the bulk of the home market for manufactures; and in most countries it is a very small home market—the

consumption of manufactures is very low, and the mere sub-
stitution of locally produced for imported manufactures
would not provide much employment or make much difference to their economies. What they need is an all-round
expansion, and this will come about (apart from valuable
exports, such as oil) only by marked improvements in
agricultural ouput, means of transport, power supplies, and
so forth. To concentrate on the rapid establishment of
manufactures is not in fact a short cut to prosperity.

These points are made in the United Nations study on
*Processes and Problems of Industrialization in Under-Developed
Countries*. For instance: 'In general, therefore, the development of agriculture, simultaneously with, if not in advance
of, manufacturing, is needed to achieve steady economic
progress and avoid structural disequilibria which may later
be the source of hardship.'[9]

The same point was made by Professor W. A. Lewis, who
can hardly be accused of being a mouthpiece of Western
capitalism, in his advice to the Gold Coast (now Ghana).[10]
'The most certain way', he wrote, 'to promote industrialization in the Gold Coast is to lay the foundation it requires by
taking vigorous measures to raise food production per
person engaged in agriculture' (para. 22); and he concluded
(para. 255) that: 'Very many years will have elapsed before
it becomes economical for the government to transfer any
large part of its resources towards industrialization'.

These views are supported, on the whole, by the economic
history of the last ten years. While most of the more advanced
countries have considerably raised their real incomes per
head, some by 20 or 30 per cent., those underdeveloped

[9] U.N., Dept. of Economic and Socia' Affairs, *Processes and Problems of
Industrialization in Under-Developed Countries* (N.Y., 1955), p. 3.
[10] *Report on Industrialization and the Gold Coast* (Accra, Govt. Printing
Dept., 1953). See also his lectures to the National Bank of Egypt:
'Aspects of Industrialization' (Cairo, 1953).

countries (e.g. Argentina, Ceylon, Chile, Cuba, Pakistan) which have made vigorous efforts to promote their industrialization have remained comparatively stagnant.

I am not of course arguing that industrialization should be ruled out. On the contrary, where conditions are suitable (as they are, for example, for steel mills in India), measures for appropriate industrialization should receive a high priority. All I am saying is that other measures (notably improvements in agricultural methods) are also needed for a general expansion; and that countries may in fact slow down their economic progress, as some have done, by devoting too much of their resources to types of industrialization for which they are not suited, or for which they are not yet prepared.

I now turn to another large and controversial subject: the sizes of farms and systems of land tenure.

In a number of countries, especially those where land is scarce, many farms are much too small to provide an adequate livelihood to the families which cultivate them. They may also be divided, as a result of a series of inheritances, into a number of small portions, some considerable distance apart. Many cultivators follow traditional practices instead of adopting improved methods which would give much higher yields. This may be due to their ignorance and their reluctance to change, but it may be partly due to the system of land tenure; for example, they may have to surrender half their produce or more as rent to their landlords, whilst themselves bearing all or most of the cost of any improvements—clearly such a system tends to discourage them from taking any measures to raise their output.

In such circumstances some radical changes seem desirable, but exactly what changes depends on local conditions. On the whole large plantations producing commodities such as rubber, tea, and sugar give considerably higher yields both per worker and per acre than smallholdings, and provide higher incomes, in the form of wages, for their workers than they would earn for themselves as smallholders. Would this apply equally to foodstuffs such as rice? Is there a case for grouping together a number of contiguous small farms into one large farm?

This would resemble the Soviet system of collective farms. If the land were fairly level, agricultural machinery could be used, setting free workers for manufacturing and other occupations. In any event the most suitable methods could be used, under the orders and supervision of trained managers; this would probably be a cheaper and more effective way of improving standards of farming than employing an army of agricultural instructors to try to persuade large numbers of peasants to change their traditional practices.

The comparative failure of collective farms in some countries (for example, China[11] and Poland) was probably due to the Government taking too high a proportion of the produce as a kind of tax, and to the absence of any close connexion between the efforts of individuals and their remuneration. But neither of these discouraging features need be present. Take, as a leading example, the Gezira scheme in the Sudan. An area of about a million acres is irrigated and leased to tenant cultivators. The latter have to follow instructions on such matters as the rotation of crops, the types of seeds planted, and the use of fertilizers; their land is ploughed for them and their cotton marketed for them by the Government; and they receive a fair share of the proceeds. Such a scheme could not be adopted everywhere (for one thing, the average Gezira farm is some 40 acres) but something on these general lines may be needed. Alternatives such as expropriating large landlords (as Mexico did), attempting to consolidate 'fragmented' holdings (as India is doing), and trying to improve methods of

[11] See Choh-ming Li, in *China Quarterly*, Jan.–Mar. 1960, pp. 41–44.

farming by agricultural instructors and demonstration farms may not have a sufficiently large and rapid effect.

It is quite possible, therefore, that some underdeveloped countries, especially those which are overpopulated, may be tempted to turn to Communism as a solution to their apparently hopeless agricultural problems. I have tried to show that some measures of compulsion and paternalism, overriding the wishes of peasants to have complete ownership of their land, may be needed; but such measures need not involve the loss of personal liberties, such as freedom of discussion and freedom of the press, or the creation of a police state, or close association with the Soviet Union or China—in other words, a country can adopt some measures which resemble those of Communist countries without becoming Communist.

The next subject to which I turn is that of the priority which should be given to social services, such as education.[12] In many underdeveloped countries the Government provides far less education, medical facilities, and other social services than in more advanced countries. The need for a great expansion in their social services seems urgent and obvious. Unfortunately most of them cannot pay for such an expansion—which involves heavy annually recurrent charges: for example, for teachers, doctors, and nurses—and at the same time carry out measures which will directly raise output. In general it seems desirable to give more priority to the latter; as output and income increase, a progressive expansion of the social services will become possible. However there is quite a possibility of conflict on this point between an aid-giving country or organization and an underdeveloped

[12] See my article 'Education and Economic Development in the Under-developed Countries', *International Affairs*, vol. 35, no. 2, Apr. 1959. I am glad to say that Professor W. A. Lewis, who is quoted in this article as saying that 'universal primary education should be an immediate objective' has changed his opinion on this question. See his letter to *The Economist*, 10 Jan. 1959, p. 118.

country which wants to spend so much on social services that the pace of its economic development would be slowed down.

Another controversial question is how far some degree of inflation may stimulate economic growth. Colonies were not able to inflate on their own, as their currencies were tied to those of their metropolitan Powers. When a colony has achieved independence, one of its first aims is usually to establish a central bank and its own currency. This enables its Government to obtain resources for development through 'deficit finance', which is less unpopular than the alternative of increasing taxes.

In some circumstances a certain amount of inflation may stimulate investment. It tends to redistribute income in favour of entrepreneurs who are likely to save and invest; the mass of the people save very little. On the other hand, continued inflation on a considerable scale may undermine confidence in the currency, and may induce the wealthier people to sell their assets and transfer the proceeds abroad into a safer currency, or to invest in assets with a quick turnover, such as trading stocks or urban buildings rather than in, for example, improvements to agricultural land. This has happened in a number of countries, for example Indonesia and Chile.

A country which engages in continuous inflation is likely to run into balance-of-payments difficulties and to seek external aid. This has happened with a number of Latin American countries. A country which participates in, say, a 'stabilization loan' would seem entitled to insist as a condition that the borrowing country should agree to follow monetary and financial policies which enable it to maintain a stable currency.

Finally, I strongly share the view that the prospects for a heavily overpopulated country such as India are gloomy unless births can be drastically reduced. This will be very difficult to achieve. A Government can keep down the death-rate but (apart from compulsory sterilization, which is unlikely to be acceptable anywhere) a Government cannot keep down the birth-rate; this can be done only if the people themselves are convinced (as they are in Japan) that it is in their own interests, and can be provided with effective means of family planning. Facilities for abortion (as in Japan) are one possibility, but might well arouse strong opposition. An oral contraceptive, which need be taken only about once a month, is perhaps the most hopeful possibility. If such a contraceptive is discovered, it is my opinion that aid to such a country should give first priority to providing money for widespread and continuous propaganda for fewer births and free distribution of the pills. Unless the outstanding economic problem of limiting births is resolutely tackled, expenditure on palliatives in such a country (whether from its own resources or from external aid) will be largely money thrown down the drain.[13]

[13] Professor A. O. Hirschman in his book *The Strategy of Economic Development* (New Haven, Conn., Yale Univ. Press, 1958), makes some observations on this point. He lays down (p. 177) these two propositions:
'Population pressure on living standards will lead to counterpressure, i.e. to activity designed to maintain or restore the traditional standard of living of the community.'
(He says that the community *learns* through wrestling successfully with new tasks. Hence:)
'The activity undertaken by the community in resisting a decline in its standards of living causes an increase in its ability to control its environment and to organize itself for development.'
On this kind of reasoning, we could say that any disaster—an earthquake or a plague of locusts, for example—is a blessing in disguise. In my opinion, this is utter nonsense. Some circumstances are favourable to economic progress and some are unfavourable; over-population as it exists in, say, China or India or Japan or Java is definitely unfavourable.
The argument that such unfavourable circumstances act as a stimulus may be answered as follows:
1. If they do, then it may take much effort and a long time merely to *restore* or *maintain* the former standards of living. These efforts could have been employed instead to *raise* standards of living.
2. The poverty of regions such as India is surely in itself sufficient stimulus to efforts for economic improvement without further adverse changes to make matters worse.

CHAPTER II

THE FLOW OF ECONOMIC AID

WHAT IS ECONOMIC AID?

THE United Nations has its own definition of economic aid. It considers that economic aid consists only of outright grants and net long-term lending, for non-military purposes, by Governments and international organizations. The chief aid-giving countries take a much broader view. In particular they include private capital investment and export credits, even for relatively short periods. This is quite understandable; it is pleasant to feel that you are helping your neighbours and at the same time increasing your own profits.

Is a definition really necessary? We all know what the underdeveloped countries need—capital, foreign exchange, technical assistance, and so forth. Why not include all that the more advanced countries provide them with, in one way or another, without arguing that some items should be labelled 'economic aid' and others should not? Personally, I think that it is important to have a definition of economic aid, and I agree with the definition adopted by the United Nations, except that I would exclude all public lending made on commercial terms.

To begin with, I think it is important to distinguish between so-called aid which has to be paid for, sooner or later, and aid which is given freely once and for all. The former leaves behind it the burden of repayment. This burden—on the country's budget and on its balance of payments—may be a heavy drag on the economy during subsequent years. The three bankers[1] who reported in April 1960 on the coming (third) Five Year Plans for India and Pakistan considered that if the foreign aid required (just over £3,000 million) were all lent at commercial rates of interest the accumulated liabilities would be intolerable.

As for private capital, this usually benefits in various ways the country in which it is invested. But it is made primarily for the benefit of the foreign shareholders, who believe that their capital will yield them a higher return there than elsewhere, and it therefore seems misleading to call private investment 'economic aid'.

Another reason for a strict definition is that it does bring out the relatively small amount of economic aid which the more advanced countries are providing. The underdeveloped countries are reluctant to point this out, lest they should be thought ungrateful and even the present flow should be reduced. But it is so. Even the United States, the chief provider, gives less than 0·5 per cent. of her national income; and since the Marshall Plan (for which Europe should surely be most grateful) the greater part of this has gone to a few countries in which the United States has special military interests.

In March 1960 the British Government published a White Paper (Cmnd. 974) on *Assistance from the United Kingdom for Overseas Development*. This White Paper arrives at a figure of about £240 million, 1¼ per cent. of the national income, as the total of economic aid provided during 1959–60. On the United Nations definition, the total would be well under half this amount. The main differences are that the White Paper includes some £100 million of private investment, £18 million disbursements from the United Kingdom

---

[1] Mr Abs, Sir Oliver Franks, and Mr Sproul, reporting to the President of the World Bank, Mr Eugene R. Black. See *The Times*, 20 Apr. 1960.

subscription to the World Bank, and £12·5 million emergency assistance (to help suppress armed revolt or terrorism) in Malaya, Kenya, and Cyprus.

I turn to a brief discussion of whether or not certain items should be counted as economic aid.

Military aid undoubtedly benefits the receiving country economically. For example, the Government of South Vietnam can use all its budget revenue for non-military purposes, as the costs of maintaining and equipping its armed forces are borne by the United States. However, it is generally agreed that military aid should be distinguished from economic aid. The United Nations defines military aid as 'transfers of military equipment, grants and loans for the purchase of military equipment or to pay military personnel and direct military expenditure for the defence of the recipient country.[2] This rules out the 'emergency assistance' included in the British White Paper. The latter of course excludes expenditure on British bases overseas, although this provides considerable income, employment, and foreign exchange: thus in Malta (with a population of 330,000) expenditure on bases has been about £20 million a year and in Singapore (with a population of 1,500,000) it has been, and still is, over £30 million a year.

Since the United Nations excludes private investment, it seems somewhat illogical that it includes long-term loans made by international bodies or national Governments on commercial terms. A leading example is loans made by the International Bank for Reconstruction and Development, commonly known as the World Bank. I do not deny for a moment that the operations of the World Bank are of great assistance to underdeveloped countries; but so is private

[2] U.N. Economic and Social Council, *International Economic Assistance to the Under-developed Countries in 1956/57: Report of the Secretary-General.* ESCOR, 26th Session, Annexes, Agenda Item 4. E3131 and Add. 1, p. 76.

investment. The World Bank charges a fairly high rate of interest, normally $1\frac{1}{4}$ per cent. above the rate at which it borrows in the market from private investors on its own bonds; at present it is charging 6 per cent. a year. It will lend only on specific projects, which it is satisfied will yield enough revenue to meet interest and repayment charges, which in any event are obligations of the borrowing Government; so far it has not had a single default. Its terms of repayment are also fairly stiff; the sum lent has to be repaid by equal annual instalments over the life of the loan. It is true that the World Bank provides very useful free services, such as making economic surveys of underdeveloped countries at their request and giving them technical assistance (mainly in connexion with projects on which they wish to borrow, or have borrowed, from it). But this does not affect the question of principle.

Similar considerations apply to loans at commercial rates from money provided by national Governments. For example, the British Colonial Development Corporation is instructed to break even on its operations, taken as a whole, and is charged full market rates for the money it borrows from the Treasury. When it lends, it charges market rates of interest, and when it engages (either alone or in partnership with private enterprise) in direct investment it expects to make the current rate of profit. It has done some valuable pioneering work, in colonies where entrepreneurs are scarce or timid, but again this does not affect the question of principle.

I agree that if loans are made free of interest then logically the market rate of interest on them should be counted as 'aid'; and similarly (for the amounts by which interest-charges are lower) with loans made below market rates. The real situation, however, may not be so clear. Such loans may be made on condition that they are spent on certain goods, such as capital equipment, supplied by the lending country. The borrowing country might have been able to buy similar goods more cheaply elsewhere, so that what it gains on the swings it may lose (or partly lose) on the roundabouts.

The United Nations excludes short-term loans, such as export credits, repayable in less than five years. This brings out the conceptual difficulty of including loans at all, for any period such as five years draws a quite arbitrary line. For example, the United Kingdom credit of £15 million to India, made in July 1958 towards the cost of the Durgapur steel mill, was in effect an export credit.[3] Had it been made for less than five years the United Nations would not have counted it as 'aid'; as it is made for longer, it does.

On this whole question, however, my quarrel is really with those publicists of national Governments who count as 'aid' the total amount authorized for loans (for example, the total capital of the Colonial Development Corporation) or who lump together authorizations and disbursements of loans over a period, without deducting repayments, rather than with the United Nations. For the latter shows only *net* lending, deducting repayments of loans (but not interest payments), so that the net amount of 'loan aid' during a period is shown as actual disbursements less any repayments (of former loans) during that period, and may be negative. Over a long period, therefore, the net amount of 'loan aid' will be comparatively small, including only loans not yet repaid and defaults (which may perhaps be regarded as aid given unintentionally). Nevertheless I consider that logically loans at market rates should not be counted as 'aid'.

The United Nations includes outright gifts of commodities

[3] It was 'tied to the purchase of specified United Kingdom exports' (Cmnd. 974, para. 32).

under aid. Examples are wheat and other agricultural products provided free (e.g. by the United States Government under Title II of Public Law 480 to meet emergency or disaster needs) and equipment provided free as part of technical assistance by Governments. It does not include, however, any government subsidies on goods provided below market prices. Nor does it include the excess payments made to less-developed countries for certain commodities bought at prices above market prices.[4] All such items should perhaps be included in 'aid', but if they were it would make little difference to the grand total.

The British White Paper of March 1960 (Cmnd. 974, para. 19) points out that:

The United Kingdom provides substantial numbers of places for overseas students at universities, technical colleges, teacher training institutions and other training establishments, including places for training in both private and nationalised industry and in commerce, nursing and many other occupations. There are at present approximately 40,000 students from overseas, most of them from the less-developed countries of the Commonwealth, undergoing a full-time course of instruction in the United Kingdom. Only a small proportion of these students are financed directly by scholarships from H.M. Government, but the United Kingdom Exchequer meets a large part of the cost of their education here in other ways.

It seems to me that these and similar costs (for example, the cost of providing free health services to temporary immigrants from underdeveloped countries) might well be included; but in fact they are not, either by the United Nations or by national Governments.

[4] A leading example is sugar, although so much of the world trade in sugar takes place under special arrangements that it is a matter for speculation what its price would be in their absence. Recently the United States was paying over 5 cents a lb. for sugar—notably over 3 million tons a year from Cuba—imported under quota arrangements, when the 'free market' price was around 3 cents a lb; and the United Kingdom pays agreed prices normally (but not always) well above 'free market' prices for agreed quotas of Commonwealth sugar.

The United Nations excludes contributions to under-developed countries by non-governmental organizations, such as the Ford, Rockefeller, and Asia Foundations. This is presumably because it regards them as private philanthropy, and not part of a deliberate national effort to provide aid. Other private contributions are also excluded; the total provided by United States religious bodies is around $400 million a year.

National Governments understandably include in their 'aid' any contributions which they make to multilateral aid, for example to the United Nations Expanded Programme of Technical Assitance. For the United Kingdom, the White Paper of March 1960 (Cmnd. 974, para. 10, Table II) estimates such contributions at £20·7 million for 1959–60. However this sum includes £18 million 'disbursements from the United Kingdom subscription to I.B.R.D.' This is in a different category from the other £2·7 million, for it is credited to the British Government, which will be repaid when the loans are repaid and will receive its share of the assets if ever the World Bank is wound up.

In order to avoid double-counting, the United Nations shows all multilateral aid separately.

It is sometimes claimed (but not in the White Paper) that releases from United Kingdom sterling balances should be counted as aid These releases undoubtedly involve 'unrequited exports' and to that extent are a strain on the British economy.[5] But the same applies to any repayment of external loans. (It applies also to the reparations currently being paid by Japan to Burma, the Philippines, Thailand, and South Vietnam.) The sterling balances belong to the overseas countries. They are in effect lent by them to the

---

[5] Unless they happen to be offset, as in the past they have been very largely offset, by increases in the sterling balances held by other countries. But this is a fortuitous matter which does not affect the argument.

United Kingdom (mostly at short-term rates, which have often been well below the rates earned by British capital invested overseas); and there is no case whatever for including releases from them in 'aid'.

THE AMOUNT OF AID: BY NON-COMMUNIST COUNTRIES

The United Nations publishes an annual report by the Secretary-General to the Economic and Social Council on

International Economic Aid to Underdeveloped Countries: Summary for 1956–57

Contributing Country or Agency	Grants	Loans ($ million)	Repayments
Bilateral Aid			
Australia	33·5	0·8	—
Belgium	—	8·0	—
Canada	23·4	—	—
France	514·3	292·8	23·7
India	3·4	—	—
Italy	6·8	—	—
Japan	0·3	—	—
Netherlands	20·9	3·5	7·4
New Zealand	5·7	0·1	—
Norway	0·9	—	—
Portugal	0·4	2·2	—
Sweden	0·3	—	—
United Kingdom	113·5	42·4	5·6
United States	1,166·5	269·9	277·3
Total	1,889·9	619·7	314·0
Multilateral Aid			
UNTA	30·6		
UNICEF	17·4		
UNKRA	20·8		
UNRWA	35·2		
IBRD	—	178·8	18·8
Total	104·0	178·8	18·8
Grand Total	1,993·9	798·5	332·8

'International Economic Assistance to the Underdeveloped Countries'; the chief figures are reproduced in its annual *Statistical Yearbook*. I have already discussed its definition of economic assistance (or aid). It defines 'underdeveloped' (or 'less developed') countries as all countries and territories in Africa, North and South America, Asia and Oceania with the exception of the Union of South Africa, Canada, the United States, Japan, Australia, and New Zealand. (It will be noted that this definition excludes Greece, Southern Italy, Yugoslavia, and the European satellites of the Soviet Union.) Aid contributed by Communist countries is excluded as the latter do not provide the United Nations with information. For 1958/9 figures see Postscript.

For 1959–60 the total amount of economic aid, as defined by the United Nations, was probably about 4 milliard U.S. dollars. The latest detailed figures, however, are for the twelve months ending 30 June 1957. A summary of these figures is reproduced above from the United Nations' *Statistical Yearbook 1958*, Table 154A.

It will be seen that the net total of economic aid for this twelve-month period was just under $2½ milliard.

As bilateral aid, the United States contributed some $1,159 million, France the equivalent of some $783 million, and the United Kingdom the equivalent of some $150 million. The contribution of France was much greater in relation to her national income than that of the United States or the United Kingdom.

The contribution of France went almost entirely to her present or former overseas territories. (Since then France has very much reduced her contribution to territories which are now independent, such as Morocco and Tunisia.)

The contribution of the United Kingdom went predominantly to the less-developed countries of the Commonwealth. During recent years 80 to 90 per cent. of American economic aid has been going to Asia, especially to countries to which the United States has been providing military aid: South Korea, South Vietnam, and Taiwan (Formosa) have between them received nearly half the grand total. During the last two or three years, however, the share of Latin America has been growing, and is likely to increase further when the Inter-American Development Bank begins operations.

Many countries which are predominantly recipients of economic aid also provide a little. For example India has been giving aid to Nepal; most countries in the Colombo Plan area provide a little technical assistance for one or more of their neighbours; and most member countries make some contribution, however small, to the various United Nations programmes and agencies.

During recent years nearly 60 per cent. of the sums expended by the United Nations on technical assistance and relief has been provided by the United States, and about 15 per cent. (mainly to UNKRA and UNRWA) by the United Kingdom. The USSR and her satellites have contributed about 3 per cent. (to the technical-assistance programmes and UNICEF).

THE AMOUNT OF AID: BY COMMUNIST COUNTRIES

Hughes and Luard give an account of Soviet aid to China.[6] The Soviet Union has been helping to plan the Chinese economy and has stressed the development of industries, especially heavy industries. She has provided plant, equipment, and technical assistance to build or rebuild a considerable number of industrial establishments—over 150 have been completed so far; together with her European satellites, she has given the services of large numbers of

[6] *Economic Development of Communist China*, ch. vii.

technical experts in various fields; and she has trained many
Chinese workers, especially in engineering, in the Soviet
Union. This aid continues, but as China is now able to rely
on her own resources, both for equipment and technical
knowledge, it is probably diminishing in amount.

It is difficult to put a monetary figure on the amount of
aid provided by one Communist country to another. We
do not know on what basis the prices of the goods supplied,
or of goods provided later in repayment, are calculated;
and the difficulty is increased when we try to translate an
estimated figure into another currency, such as dollars or
sterling.

Hughes and Luard[7] quote the Chinese Minister of
Finance as saying in July 1957 that, since the founding of
the People's Republic, Soviet aid had amounted to 5,294
million yuan, and they add 'about £750 million'. The
Minister of Finance may have exaggerated, in order to
please the Soviet Union, for example by including Russian
credits authorized but not yet drawn upon; other estimates
are substantially lower for this period. No doubt this aid
considerably speeded up the industrialization of China, but
even if we accept the figure of £750 million, it was not very
large in relation to China's needs. As Hughes and Luard
point out,[8] it compares somewhat unfavourably with the
amount of external aid provided to India during her first
and second Five-Year Plans. Moreover, most of it consisted
of loans. Repayment, in the form of Chinese materials and
other products, began some years ago and accounts for the
recent large export surplus[9] on China's trade with the Soviet
Union.

---

[7] *Economic Development of Communist China*, p. 77.
[8] Ibid.
[9] About $220 million in 1957 and $250 million in 1958. (*The Times*, 23
Sept. 1959.)

Although China is predominantly a recipient of aid, she also provides aid. She agreed in 1953 and 1955 to give North Korea and North Vietnam respectively $320 million each in grants.[10] She has also provided assistance, on a much smaller scale, to certain other Asian countries. She has, for instance, made grants (or non-repayable credits) to Cambodia in 1956 (to the value of about $11 million); to Nepal in 1956 (about $8·8 million) and in 1960 (about $21 million); to Ceylon in 1957 (about $12 million); to Burma in 1957 (about $1·8 million);[11] and also to Indonesia.

The aid provided by Communist countries to non-Communist countries is discussed by Mr Alec Nove in his book *Communist Economic Strategy*.[12] It has been much publicized, but as Nr Nove points out,[13] the actual amount disbursed up to March 1959 was 'at the most only $750 million' and from this the repayments made, for example by Egypt and Burma should be deducted. The total of $2·5 milliard for Sino-Soviet Bloc Aid from January 1954 to March 1959[14] includes the above $750 million; the remainder consists of credits which will be drawn upon over the next few years. This total includes military aid,[15] and most of it consists of interest-bearing loans or credits from the Soviet Union; although interest-rates are low (mostly $2\frac{1}{2}$ per cent. a year on loans repayable over twelve years), these loans or credits have to be repaid. Mr Nove estimates the composition of this total as follows:

[10] *New York Times*, 27 May 1956.

[11] 'The Weapon of Trade' by Yuan-li Wu in *Problems of Communism*, vol. ix, no. 1, Jan.-Feb. 1960.

[12] Washington, D.C., National Planning Association, 1959.

[13] Ibid. p. 54.

[14] Notably some $350 million for arms, most of which were delivered some years ago, to Egypt and Syria.

[15] Ibid. p. 55.

Sino-Soviet Bloc Aid
($ million)

Egypt	620
Syria	325
Iraq	255
Yemen	50
Afghanistan	160
Burma	40
India	310
Ceylon	50
Indonesia	360
Cambodia	30
Argentina	104
All others (excl. Yugoslavia)*	36
	2,340
Yugoslavia	160
Total (incl. Yugoslavia)	2,500

* Ethiopia, Iran, Turkey, Nepal, Iceland, and Brazil.

It will be seen that the amount of Soviet aid is usually much exaggerated.[16] 'It has become customary in the West', writes Mr Nove[17], 'to stress the vast extent of Soviet aid to underdeveloped countries, the object being partly to dramatize the non-military dangers to the West, and partly to persuade reluctant congressmen to vote foreign aid programmes'. Whether or not the exaggeration is deliberate, I am convinced that the best course in such matters is to state what seem to be the facts, regardless of whether they appear to favour or to hinder any particular line of propaganda.

Soviet aid may be comparatively small at present (although naturally it is directed mainly to places where it is most likely to help Communist propaganda or to annoy the West) but is it likely to increase substantially in the near future? Mr Nove thinks not. He says that while the rate of Soviet deliveries, on the basis of existing commitments,

---

[16] 'Current estimates are that Soviet aid to non-communist under-developed areas since 1955 has averaged about $700 million per year'. (Paul G. Hoffman, *One Hundred Countries, One and One Quarter Billion People* (Washington D.C., 1960), p. 29.)

[17] Ibid. p. 54.

should show an upward tendency over the next few years, it is doubtful whether the rate at which new credits are negotiated will rise much, except for 'a few selected countries', such as Iraq, 'when the political dividends are tempting'.[18]

He bases his view mainly on his belief that the Sino-Soviet bloc will give priority to maintaining their own rates of economic growth and will not be able to spare much more than they are providing now, in the form of capital equipment and other goods and services, for non-communist countries.

IS MORE AID NEEDED?

From the standpoint of the underdeveloped countries, the amount of economic aid received is small in relation to their needs. A considerable share of the total has been going to a few countries: those in which the United States has special military interests (notably South Korea, South Vietnam and Taiwan) or which she is especially concerned to prevent from turning Communist (such as Cambodia and Laos, Bolivia, and Guatemala); French territories in Africa, especially Algeria; and Israel. Most of the others have been receiving comparatively little.

The United Nations report (E/3131) to the twenty-sixth session of the Economic and Social Council in 1958 lists twenty countries with per caput incomes of less than $100. Together they received net economic aid of $1,004 million in 1956–7. Of this total, $336 million went to South Korea, $246 million to South Vietnam, $41 million to Cambodia, $49 million to Laos, and $34 million to Libya. The remaining fifteen countries, with a combined population of over 670 million, received only $400 million, about 60 cents a head. India received only 10 cents a head.

[18] *Communist Economic Strategy*, pp. 55 f.

Eighteen countries with per caput incomes between $100 and $200 received net economic aid of $464 million. Of this total, $111 million went to Taiwan, $24 million to Bolivia, $26 million to Guatemala, $79 million to Morocco, and $50 million to Tunisia. The remaining thirteen countries, with a combined population of 175 million, received $174 million, about $1.00 a head.

The amount of aid received by most underdeveloped countries was equivalent to some 1 per cent., or less, of their national incomes—hardly enough to have a very significant effect in stimulating their economic growth.

It is true that the amount of net economic aid now being provided is greater, perhaps by a quarter, than in 1956–7. But populations have grown, and prices have risen; fundamentally the situation is much the same as it was then.

How much aid is needed? The combined population of non-Communist underdeveloped countries is over 1,200 million and their average income per head is about $130 a year. In order to raise their incomes forthwith to substantially higher levels, say an average of $200 a year per head, something over $85 milliard a year would be needed. This is obviously quite out of the question. Nor do most of the underdeveloped countries seek continuous large-scale charity. What they want is external aid sufficient to give their own economies a dynamic upward trend.

Further increases in wealth are easier for a nation, as for an individual, when it has already travelled a certain distance along this road. Higher incomes make possible not only a larger amount of saving and investment but also a larger proportion than incomes which are so low that they afford little margin for saving after providing for subsistence needs. The development of an adequate 'infrastructure' of roads and other transport facilities, supplies of electric power, educated and trained workers makes it much easier to raise output per worker in all fields of economic activity. Economic growth in various fields provides better facilities ('external economies') to both existing and new establishments and expands the purchasing-power of the home market.

This phenomenon has been called 'the take-off into self-sustained growth;'[19] and it is often urged that economic aid should be of an amount and nature which will eventually enable the recipient country to go ahead under its own steam.

This seems sensible. I disagree, however, with the implications of the view, which is at present fashionable, that what a country needs to reach the 'take-off' stage is an annual investment equal to a certain percentage, say 15 per cent., of its national income.[20]

One reason for my disagreement is that the real national incomes per head of underdeveloped countries differ widely. Those of the richer countries of Asia, Africa, and Latin America are three, four, or five times as high as those of

---

[19] This is the title of an article by W. W. Rostow in the *Economic Journal*, vol. lxvi, no. 261, Mar. 1956, pp. 25–48.

[20] This view has been expressed recently in *The Economist*, 26 Mar. 1960, p. 1263: 'Briefly, the new theory of growth starts with the traditional static economy where, perhaps not more than five per cent of national income is devoted to productive investment—a percentage which does no more than keep the economy stable. It is in no sense a lever of expansion. The decisive break-through towards growth becomes possible with modern science, technology and industry and the new openings for investment which they provide. In very general terms, one can say that when annual investment in such an economy approaches three times the static level of five per cent, a new threshold is reached.

As, very roughly, three units of investment should produce one extra unit of income, annual investment running at around fifteen per cent of national income can thus, if wisely channelled, create a five per cent annual increase in national income. Even allowing for an annual 2 per cent rise in population, like that of contemporary India, a five per cent annual increase in income allows for some growth in consumption and still leaves over a margin for further investment and hence for "take-off" into self-sustaining growth.'

their poorest neighbours. Yet the costs of particular capital assets—a certain mileage of roads, a power-station of given capacity, school buildings for so many children—are much the same in all these countries. Hence the same percentage of national income invested provides a much greater amount of capital assets in a richer country than it does in a poorer one. If a richer country and a poorer country both manage to save the same percentage (say 10 per cent.) of their national incomes, then the external aid needed to bring this percentage up to the 'take-off' level (say 15 per cent.) would be several times greater, relatively to its population, for the former. This seems absurd. On the whole, a poorer country needs more external aid per head than a richer country, and not only one-third or one-quarter as much.

I disagree with this view itself, apart from its implications. Economic growth does not only depend on the amount (or percentage) of investment. It depends on the character and abilities of the people, especially on their capacity to learn and apply improved methods of production; and on the numbers and qualities of their entrepreneurs. It depends on the provision of adequate incentives to effort and investment (including land reform, where needed); on general economic and social policy; on the ability and honesty of Ministers and civil servants; on social customs; and, over a period, the fortunes of some countries may be considerably affected by marked favourable or adverse movements in their terms of trade.

All this seems very obvious, and no doubt those who stress the importance of investment would say that they are merely simplifying by assuming other factors to be more or less equal. But in fact they are not equal. For example, in some countries large increases in output have been brought about at relatively little cost by discovering and planting higher-yielding crop varieties, by better breeding and feeding of animals, by stamping out plant and animal diseases, by the use of powered vessels for fishing and by turning fish into fish-meal for export, by technical training, and so forth. In some countries a great deal could be done on these and similar lines. On the other hand, some investment (for example, in certain large-scale irrigation schemes, in some steel mills, in the East African groundnuts scheme) has yielded little return.

One has only to look around the world to see that the attainment of a certain level of income per head, or of a certain level of investment, is no guarantee whatever of sustained economic growth. India is striving hard to raise her income per head from about £25 to £30 a year. What about Ceylon, which has been stagnating on an income of some £40 a head per year? Why should India necessarily do any better? What about Argentina, which Professor Rostow thought had 'taken off' around 1935?[21] During most of the post-war period Argentina made very little progress, owing to President Perón's attempt to speed up industrialization at the expense of agriculture, and to other factors such as adverse terms of trade. If the percentage of income invested is the chief criterion, what about Laos, a country which has been receiving grants equal to over 20 per cent. of its income during recent years? No doubt it will be said that for economic growth other conditions also must be present. That is precisely what I am urging.

It may be that many people in underdeveloped countries would prefer to take life as easily as they can rather than to work harder and save more in order, eventually, to raise their standards of living. Nobody can blame them if they do. But a country is not likely to make rapid economic progress unless the mass of the people have a strong desire, an enthusiasm, to bring it about.

[21] *Economic Journal*, Mar. 1960, p. 31

If this enthusiasm can be aroused—and this may need a lot of propaganda—there are hundreds of things that people can do to help themselves. They can improve their homes, their diet, their appearance, by learning such arts as carpentry, cookery, dressmaking; they can even learn to build themselves new and better houses. The under-employed labour can be transformed into a national asset by inducing people to give their labour freely (under expert supervision) for the benefit of their village communities in projects such as making or improving local roads, putting up schools and other communal buildings, sinking tube-wells, and digging irrigation trenches.[22] Those who can read and write can teach others to do so. Those farmers who have tried out improved methods can convert others to adopt them. A whole village can become alive and dynamic instead of squalid and dead.

Whatever may be the relative stress laid on different factors, however, it seems clear that most countries have been and are receiving too little economic aid to make possible a continued and progressive increase in their output per head. Apart from a few favoured countries, which I have mentioned, external aid has amounted to only one to two dollars a year (or less) per head of their populations—around 1 per cent. or less of their national incomes. It is not enough, as is shown by the relatively small rise in the real incomes per head of most underdeveloped countries during recent years compared with the relatively large rise in most of the more advanced countries.[23]

[22] Unfortunately the 'community development' projects in India and elsewhere have accomplished less than was hoped, perhaps because of too much governmental supervision and red tape.

[23] The view that most underdeveloped countries have only a limited 'absorptive capacity' for external aid is discussed on pp. 115–17 below.

CHAPTER III

INTERNATIONAL TRADE

EXPORT EARNINGS

THE belief that international trade consists mainly of the exchange of manufactured goods from the industrial countries against primary products from the underdeveloped countries is quite wrong. If we exclude the trade of the Communist countries (just over 10 per cent. of the total), more than half the remainder is trade among the industrial countries themselves. Some 10 per cent is trade among the underdeveloped countries themselves, and less than one-third is trade between them and the industrial countries.

Nor is it correct to suppose that most of the world's primary products are produced in the underdeveloped countries. On the contrary the industrial countries produce over half the foodstuffs and over two-thirds of the raw materials (as well as some 80 per cent. of the manufactures). As the industrial countries have only about one-third of the world's population, these figures reflect their much greater output per head.

Some major exports of primary products come mainly from the industrial, or more accurately, the wealthier countries; for example, cereals (except rice), meat, and dairy products; wool and cotton; timber, woodpulp, and newsprint. Synthetic rubber, produced in the industrial countries, is a close substitute for natural rubber, and synthetic fibres are a close substitute for natural fibres such as cotton and silk.

What is true is that the underdeveloped countries, with

very few exceptions (notably Hong Kong and India), export almost entirely primary products, and that at least four-fifths of their exports go to the industrial countries.

Many underdeveloped countries export a considerable proportion of their output, and therefore changes in their export earnings have significant effects on their economies. A marked fall may bring about a local depression and slow down the pace of development; a marked rise may do the opposite. Even a country such as India, which exports only a small proportion of its output, depends largely on its export earnings to pay for its imports of capital goods and other requirements.

The export earnings of underdeveloped countries do fluctuate quite considerably. Over the period 1901 to 1950 the year-to-year fluctuations of export proceeds for eighteen primary products exported by certain underdeveloped countries averaged nearly 23 per cent.[1] During 1950 to 1957, also, 'a high degree of instability in export earnings' was commonly experienced by most countries exporting primary products (other than oil); although the extent of annual fluctuations was smaller than before the war, ranging from 10 to 15 per cent. for most countries (but reaching 21 per cent. for Malaya).[2]

It is sometimes said that fluctuations (notably those arising from booms and depressions) in the economic activity of the industrial countries dominate the export earnings of the underdeveloped countries. For example, Professor Ragnar Nurkse,[3] quoting the figures for 1901 to 1950 mentioned above, and noting that fluctuations in the volume of

[1] U.N. Dept. of Economic Affairs, *Instability in Export Markets of Under-Developed Countries* (N.Y. 1952), p. 40.

[2] U.N., *World Economic Survey 1958*, p. 59.

[3] 'Trade Fluctuations and Buffer Policies of Low-Income Countries', *Kyklos*, vol. ix, 1958, Fasc. 2.

exports (which were somewhat greater than fluctuations in price) more often than not moved in the same direction as prices, larger volumes accompanying higher prices and conversely, claims that these figures furnish 'conclusive proof —if proof were needed—that the export fluctuations of primary producing countries originate in the world's industrial centers. More specifically, they seem to originate in the general swings of investment in fixed capital.'

There is no doubt that the industrial countries can potentially exert a dominant influence, through changes in their demand for imports, on the world prices and export proceeds of most primary products. To what extent they in fact do so is another question.

They may have done so, owing to the frequency and magnitude of their booms and depressions, until recent times. The outstanding example is the great depression of 1930 to 1933, when the world prices of most primary products fell heavily, some by more than half.

It seems, however, that the situation has changed since the war. The general view is that another world slump at all comparable to the great depression will not be allowed to take place. So far, there have been no major booms or depressions and, apart from a sharp but short-lived rise during the Korean War (1950–51), the demand for imports of most primary products by the industrial countries has been expanding fairly steadily.

During the three recessions in the United States of 1948–9, 1953–4, and 1957–8, its volume of imports fell by only 5, $2\frac{1}{2}$, and $1\frac{1}{2}$ per cent. respectively. This is in striking contrast to the pre-war pattern: for example, in 1938 a fall of only 4 per cent. in American consumption was accompanied by a fall of 25 per cent. in the volume of imports.

The 1957–8 recession in the United States had its

parallel in Western Europe (including the United Kingdom). Although industrial output remained fairly stable in Western Europe,[4] this was in striking contrast to the rapid rise, of some 30 per cent., which had been taking place (for the area as a whole) since 1953.

The consequence was that some underdeveloped countries, which had come to expect a continuous expansion in their export earnings, were confronted instead with a fall. The average prices of primary products fell by some 6 per cent. The export proceeds of eighty-two countries exporting mainly primary products fell from a peak of $30 milliard in 1957 to somewhat over $28 milliard in 1958[5] (but have since recovered).

It does not follow, however, that changes in the export earnings of primary products were due mainly to changes in demand by the industrial countries, either during the post-war period as a whole or during the 1957–8 recession. The prices of some primary products have risen sharply while the prices of others have remained fairly stable, or have fallen, during any particular year, while a primary product which has experienced a marked rise in price has later had a marked fall, or conversely. All this suggests that the reasons for changes in the export proceeds of any particular commodity can be found only by studying the conditions affecting that particular commodity, and should not be attributed to general fluctuations in the economic activity of the industrial countries. Changes in supply may have been more influential than changes in demand; for example, the supply of some major primary products (such as oil and coffee) had considerably expanded by 1958.

[4] In the United States the Federal Reserve Board's index of industrial production started to move downward in September 1957. It fell by 13 per cent. to a low point in August 1958 and then recovered, reaching its pre-recession level in February 1959.

[5] U.N., *World Economic Survey 1958*, p. 217.

The *World Economic Survey 1958* discusses this question. It concludes (p. 48) that during the post-war period

in only a minority of primary commodities, particularly the mineral raw materials, have cyclical variations in demand within the industrial countries dominated the pattern of short-period fluctuations in both volume and price. The behaviour of prices and volume of trade of most foodstuffs, and of prices—though not of volume of trade—of textile fibres, has been heavily influenced by the instability of supply conditions and has not conformed to any systematic cyclical pattern.[6]

These considerations apply also to the controversy about the terms of trade. Some claim that these are less favourable to underdeveloped countries than they should be, owing to the dominant part played by industrial countries in the demand for their exports. I do not think there are any grounds for this view.

The issue is often confused by taking the price-ratio between manufactured goods and primary products to reflect the terms of trade between industrial and under-developed countries. This is not correct. Some primary products are exported mainly by industrial countries, and some underdeveloped countries spend a considerable proportion of their export earnings on fuel (mainly oil) and raw materials and even foodstuffs. The terms of trade of particular underdeveloped countries have moved very differently from one another. For example until 1958 those countries exporting commodities such as oil and coffee enjoyed a considerable improvement (since about 1948) in their terms of trade, while others (Argentina, for instance) did not. Again, it has been pointed out that during the

[6] See also the study by A. J. Brown: *Impact of Fluctuations in Economic Activity in Industrial Countries on International Commodity Trade.* E/CN. 13/L. 68. (N.Y., U.N. Economic and Social Council, 1960, mimeo.). One of Professor Brown's conclusions is that 'changes in industrial activity do not provide more than a part of the explanation of short-term changes in real prices of primary commodities' (p. 35).

1957–8 recession the terms of trade moved unfavourably (by about 10 per cent.) to primary products relatively to manufactures. The short answer to this is that in 1955–7 the prices of primary products, relatively to the prices of manufactures, were 25 to 33 per cent. higher—the exact percentage depending on the method of calculation—than they were in 1928, before the great depression.[7]

Nevertheless it is beyond dispute that the export earnings of underdeveloped countries do fluctuate quite considerably from time to time. They would clearly be in a better position if their export earnings could both be made more stable (but expanding) and substantially raised. It is urged from time to time that the industrial countries should take measures to bring this about. That is the meaning of the view that the underdeveloped countries need 'trade, not aid'.

Undoubtedly most, perhaps all, underdeveloped countries would prefer a substantial rise in their export earnings to an equivalent amount of aid. The former would carry no implication of charity and would have no strings attached, so that it would not offend their national dignity and pride. It is far from certain, however, that higher and more stable export earnings would lead to corresponding increases in expenditure on development. Whereas aid is normally channelled into specific developmental projects, higher export earnings might well be spent, in practice, largely on current consumption, to raise immediately the present low standards of living.

In any event it seems out of the question that 'trade' could replace 'aid'. An increase of over 10 per cent. in their export earnings would be needed merely to compensate underdeveloped countries for the loss of the economic aid which they are now receiving, and it is generally agreed

[7] *World Economic Survey 1958*, p. 19 n.

that this should be substantially increased. There are no practicable means by which their export earnings could be permanently raised, over the next few years, by enough to replace economic aid. I shall consider what measures the more advanced countries might take to make the export earnings of underdeveloped countries higher and more stable, and also what measures they might take themselves, but it seems clear that such measures could be only a supplement to economic aid and not a substitute for it.

INTERNATIONAL COMMODITY AGREEMENTS

When the world price of a primary product is falling, whether owing to increased supplies or to a fall in demand, a country which provides a large proportion of the total exports may be able to check the fall in price, at least for a time, by reducing its own exports. This is what Brazil did for coffee in the 1930's; she reduced her own exports and accumulated large stocks (some of which she destroyed). It is expensive, however, for one country alone to bear the whole burden of restricting exports, and the long-run consequence may be to make it possible for other countries to maintain or expand theirs: Brazil, which used to provide over 60 per cent. of world exports of coffee, now provides only about 45 per cent.

A country which supplies only a small proportion of the total exports is almost powerless to affect the world price by independent action.

Clearly what is needed, if world prices are not to be allowed to take their course, is combined action by all the exporting countries.

If all the exporting countries, or at least all the major ones, agree to co-operate, they can do more than put a brake on falls in price. They can reduce the amplitude of price-fluctuations, both upwards and downwards, by adjusting the total volume of exports to changes in demand by the importing countries. In addition, they can probably make their export earnings greater than they would be otherwise.

This last point needs some explanation. Suppose, to take a hypothetical example, that 180,000 tons of tin a year would sell for £600 a ton whereas 150,000 tons would sell for £800 a ton. By reducing their combined exports from 180,000 tons to 150,000 tons, the tin-producing countries could raise their total export earnings from £108 million to £120 million. (This, of course, applies only over a certain price range; to keep to my hypothetical example, to raise the price of tin to £1,000 a ton might involve restricting exports to, say, 100,000 tons a year, giving annual export earnings of only £100 million.)

Whether it would be in the long-run interests of exporting countries to maximize their export earnings by restricting exports and raising prices depends on circumstances. It might pay them to do so for tin, as known deposits are limited and there is no close substitute. For some other commodities, a moderate price policy might be more advantageous; it would encourage the growth of consumption and would check the use of existing substitutes and the search for new ones. The more efficient producing countries often favour a moderate price policy; for example, the Federation of Malaya (faced with growing competition from synthetic rubber) for rubber, and Cuba (wishing to check the expansion of high-cost sugar-growing, both beet and cane, in some consuming countries) for sugar.

In practice, however, the exporting countries are not left entirely to their own devices. The post-war view is that importing countries should be represented on the Councils of international commodity agreements, and they are so represented on the Wheat Council, the Sugar Council, and the Tin Council. They help the agreements to work more smoothly (for example, by providing estimates of their own future demands) but they are there primarily to protect the interests of consumers. They may help in trying to smooth out marked temporary price-fluctuations and in trying to prevent prices from falling below an agreed minimum or 'floor', but in return they want the agreement to aim at keeping prices below an agreed maximum or 'ceiling'. The Sugar Agreement provides that exporting (but not importing) countries should each hold stocks of not less than $12\frac{1}{2}$ per cent. of their basic export tonnage immediately before the start of the new crop; 'such stocks shall be earmarked to fill increased requirements of the free market and used for no other purpose without the consent of the Council'. The Tin Agreement has a buffer stock to prevent prices rising above the ceiling (as well as falling below the floor); the costs of the buffer stock are borne entirely by the exporting countries.

It seems clear that the importing countries would not permit a producers' monopoly to maximize export earnings at their expense, even though this would mean a transfer of wealth from richer (consumers) to poorer (producers). The attitude of the United States was made plain in 1951 when she complained of 'price gouging' (although in fact higher prices were due entirely to increased demand) and stopped buying tin for a period, and again in 1954 when she held a detailed enquiry into the reasons for the high price of coffee.

Two questions may be asked about international commodity agreements: are they desirable? And are they practicable?

It is certainly desirable to smooth out large fluctuations, first upwards and then downwards or conversely, in commodity prices. But it is seldom desirable to keep the price of a commodity completely stable. Price changes play a leading part in a free economy; they guide both producers and consumers to make the best use of resources. For example, if the demand for a commodity is growing, a rising price encourages producers to expand their output and to seek new sources of supply. If costs of production are falling (owing for example to higher-yielding planting material) a falling price will pass on the benefit to consumers and encourage consumption to expand. If there is general inflation, there is no reason why primary products should be excluded from the general rise in prices. An international commodity agreement is desirable only in so far as those controlling it make a correct diagnosis of the situation, and can distinguish between short-period fluctuations and long-term trends; if they judge wrongly they delay necessary adjustments, making them more severe when they have to come.

The chief measures by which supply can be adjusted to changes in demand are variations in the amount of exports, and purchases or sales by a buffer stock.

It is difficult to get all the exporting countries to join an international agreement which (as in the sugar and tin agreements) gives each of them an export quota and requires all of them to raise or reduce their volume of exports by a given percentage on the instructions of the Council. Some may believe that they are entitled to a larger share of world exports than others are willing to concede them. But if some countries stay outside the agreement and are free to expand their exports while member countries are restricting theirs, the scheme is likely to collapse.

If there is a buffer stock (as there is for tin) it may be expensive. Most commodities (unlike tin) require ample storage space and are subject to deterioration and damage while in store. The costs of a buffer stock, including interest on the capital locked up in it, may amount to 10 per cent. or more a year of its value.

Then there is the problem of 'differentials'. Most primary products are far from homogeneous. Unlike sugar and tin, they have different varieties and qualities, the prices of which vary considerably (in relation to one another) as time goes on. Exporting countries may not be willing to accept the ruling of an international body (notably under a multilateral contract scheme, such as that for wheat) on a 'fair' maximum or minimum price for their special varieties or qualities.

These obstacles are formidable. This is shown by the fact that at present there are only three international commodity agreements—for wheat, sugar, and tin—and each of these took several years to negotiate.[8]

NATIONAL STABILIZATION MEASURES

Many underdeveloped countries rely largely on their export earnings from some primary product for which there is no international commodity agreement. As a rule, such a country cannot significantly affect the world price of its chief export (or exports), or could do so only at too heavy a cost.

A marked fall in its export earnings may take place for any of several reasons. It may have a bad harvest, while other countries exporting that product do not. The demand for that product may fall, owing to a recession in importing countries or to the greater use of cheaper or more suitable substitutes. Its world price may fall, either for these reasons or owing to greater technical progress, reducing costs, in other exporting countries.

[8] A fuller disussion of these questions will be found in my essay 'On Stabilizing the Prices of Primary Products' in *The Colombo Plan and other essays* (London, RIIA, 1956), pp. 55–75.

A marked fall in export earnings is likely to cause a local depression. Incomes will fall, public revenue will fall, and some development projects may have to be postponed or curtailed. What measures can such a country take, independently, to prevent these consequences or at least to make them less severe? It should build up adequate reserves, including reserves of foreign exchange, when times are relatively good, on which it can draw to tide it over a lean period of reduced export earnings. By drawing on its reserves, the Government will be able to maintain both its normal and its developmental expenditure. There will be no need to make any substantial reductions in the volume of imports (including imports needed for developmental projects); such reductions would not only harm the country itself, they would also adversely affect the countries supplying it with imports and would tend to spread its depression to them.

Should its reserves be insufficient to tide it over the lean period, a country may be able to supplement them (if it has its own central bank) by creating more money. Such 'deficit finance' is more likely to be successful, and not to weaken confidence in the currency and to reduce saving, if the country has followed a policy of budgeting for surpluses during previous years. Another way of supplementing its reserves is by raising stabilization loans from international bodies (notably the International Monetary Fund) or from other countries.

Measures to soften a local depression will be more effective if opposite measures have been taken to prevent investment and expenditure from becoming too great during a period of comparative boom. The greater the debauch, the greater the headache; the more marked the boom, the more severe the depression.

Some measures available to industrial countries would

not be very effective in underdeveloped countries. For example, if the latter have only rudimentary money markets, changes in short-term rates of interest may have little effect. The same applies to devices such as changes in 'investment allowances' in countries where there is relatively little industry; and changes in social insurance contributions are inapplicable to countries too poor to afford social insurance.

However, various measures are available. Many underdeveloped countries have a central bank. If the commercial banks are required to keep a percentage of their deposits with the central bank, this percentage can be reduced when a local depression seems to be threatening. Again, if a local depression seems likely to be accompanied by considerable unemployment, Governments and other public authorities can provide other employment by introducing (or speeding up) developmental projects which have already been planned but have been kept in reserve for such a contingency.

The most important measure available, however, is probably changes in taxation. The yields of taxes at given rates will be higher when times are good than when times are bad, but in addition the rates of certain taxes can be varied. There would probably be considerable opposition to raising rates of income tax when times were good, and the Government had a substantial budget surplus, and there is usually a considerable time-lag before changes in rates of income tax (reductions during an actual or threatened depression) take effect. The only taxes on consumption with a high enough yield for changes in them to have a significant effect are usually taxes on staple foodstuffs (or other commodities widely consumed), and it is arguable that if there are taxes on such commodities they should be kept low, even during relatively good times.

The obvious candidate for changes in rates of tax is the principal export product (or products). Such changes take effect immediately, and if the export earnings form a substantial part of the national income, they affect incomes and expenditures not only in the export industries but throughout the economy. Many countries follow this practice. The Pakistan export duty on cotton was raised from (the equivalent of) 3.50 U.S. cents per lb. to 23.09 cents in November 1950 (during the Korean boom) and then reduced to 6.93 cents in October 1952. Two or three countries have sliding-scale export duties laid down in advance, instead of varying them *ad hoc*. For instance the export duty levied on rubber by the Federation of Malaya is nil when the price is below 60 (Malayan) cents a pound, 5 per cent. within the range of 60 cents to a dollar, and rises steeply and progressively when the price exceeds a dollar.

Countries with multiple exchange rates (mostly in South America) obtain the same result by giving their exporters an unfavourable rate of exchange (the difference going to the Government) when the world price of the commodity is high, and a more favourable rate when it is low.

An alternative is to set up a State Marketing Board, to which all producers must sell and which has a monopoly of exporting the product. The Board keeps prices to the growers fairly stable but usually well below the equivalent export prices. Hence variations in export prices affect government revenue but have little repercussion on the producers. Leading examples are the Ghana Cocoa Marketing Board and (for rice) the State Agricultural Marketing Board of Burma.

The view that special taxation of the export industries is morally wrong need not be taken too seriously; a Government is entitled to raise revenue as best it can. On economic grounds there seems no objection, provided that the net return to producers is not reduced so much that investment and expansion by the export industries are unduly checked. Certainly for a number of countries these variable export duties (or exchange rates, or Marketing Board profits) are a valuable stabilizing measure which softens local depressions.

I have assumed throughout the above discussion that the fall in export earnings is only temporary. If, on the contrary, it is due to some lasting change, such as the discovery of a substitute which consumers prefer to the export product in question, then more far-reaching and long-term adjustments are needed. If they are not made, reserves will be depleted but foreign-exchange earnings will remain inadequate; deficit finance will lead to continuous inflation; or still more stabilization loans will be needed but will prove difficult or impossible to repay.

If possible, new sources of export earnings should be developed. This was done, for example, by Chile after her natural nitrate had been largely replaced by synthetic nitrate and by Japan after the heavy reduction in her earnings from natural silk, her chief export, after 1929. Otherwise, adjustment will involve a painful reduction in standards of living (and, so far as possible, increased saving) to bring the balance of payments into equilibrium.

WHAT CAN THE INDUSTRIAL COUNTRIES DO?

What most underdeveloped countries would like best of all would be an undertaking by the chief importing countries to buy unlimited (or at least 'adequate') amounts of their products at 'fair' prices. More often than not, the prices which they considered 'fair' would be well above those that would result from the free play of market forces. Hence such undertakings would lead to large and constantly growing stocks of these products in the importing countries. This is a liability which the latter are not willing to accept.

The United States does help her own farmers in this way.

But she is not prepared to do the same for the farmers of other countries. And even if she were, the conditions which she enforces on her own farmers—price reductions or acreage restrictions as stocks accumulate—would be resented by the exporting countries if applied to them, for the result, after a time, would be sharp falls in their export earnings.

It is true that some special arrangements are at present in force. For example, the United States—contrary to her own principles of non-discriminatory trade—pays prices equivalent to those received by her own sugar growers for her imported sugar, but to certain countries only, and for limited amounts (corresponding to her import requirements and therefore not leading to the accumulation of stocks). The United Kingdom provides a sheltered if limited market for certain imports from the Commonwealth; this was one reason why she did not immediately join the European Economic Community of the Six, as in my view she should have done.

But any general expansion of such special arrangements (subject, presumably, to safeguards by the industrial countries to protect their own farmers) is out of the question. The markets of the industrial countries are not large enough to absorb all the imports that would be forthcoming at 'fair' prices. Either stocks would continually grow or a world-wide system of import quotas would be needed. The progress made during recent years towards greater freedom of trade and the removal of barriers and controls (such as import quotas) would be reversed.

In the non-Communist world of private trading, prices reflect the conditions of supply and demand. When a commodity becomes scarcer, or the demand for it increases, its price tends to rise, stimulating greater production. Conversely, improved methods of cultivation or higher yields lead to lower prices and stimulate consumption. These

valuable functions of a free market would be largely destroyed if there were a system of agreed prices. Hence, in
general, the industrial countries prefer to provide economic
aid for specific purposes rather than to wrap up their aid in
prices above market levels to particular groups of producers
or to attempt to fix prices for a wide range of commodities.

The Communist countries can readily pay special prices,
if they wish, for their foreign trade is carried on by their
Governments. They import only a small proportion of the
total world exports of primary products, but they can select
for this type of assistance countries with relatively small
exports, so that the cost is not too great, where the political
or propaganda returns seem worth while.

The available evidence suggests, however, that they have
not in fact done a great deal on these lines.[9] Some exporting countries have made arrangements which seemed
favourable at the time but now seem less attractive. A considerable part of Egypt's present and future cotton exports
is tied up in paying for the arms received some years ago
from the Soviet Union and Czechoslovakia. China began by
paying some 50 per cent. above world prices for Ceylon
rubber (sending rice in exchange) but subsequent changes
in the terms of this agreement have been less satisfactory to
Ceylon. Burma was glad to sell rice at favourable prices
to China some years ago, but was not so pleased with the
goods offered by China in return, or by the re-export of
her rice to her traditional markets.

However, the extent to which Communist countries have
or have not conferred real benefits on underdeveloped
countries in the sphere of trade is not very relevant. The
main point is that their imports from such countries are

[9] See, for instance, J. S. Berliner, *Soviet Economic Aid* (N.Y., Praeger,
and London, OUP, for Council on Foreign Relations, 1958) and A. Nove
and D. Donnelly, *Trade with Communist Countries* (London, Hutchinson
for Institute of Economic Affairs, 1960).

relatively small. Any substantial help must come from the non-Communist countries. I have argued that the latter are most unlikely to pay special prices, except for limited amounts of certain products (such as sugar) from a few countries. Is there any other way in which they could help?

They already give the greatest of all benefits, free and unrestricted entry to their markets, to most exports from underdeveloped countries. The chief exceptions are summarized in the following paragraph.

Nearly all of them protect their own farmers, but this affects mainly the foodstuffs of temperate climates (such as wheat, meat, and dairy products) so that with a few exceptions, such as Argentina, the less developed countries are not injured. A number of countries (both developed and underdeveloped) produce sugar for themselves at a higher cost than they could import it; a general free-trade policy for sugar (most unlikely now that so many growers are protected or subsidized) would probably benefit the more efficient exporting countries (such as Cuba) even if at the same time all preferential import arrangements were swept away. The acreage restrictions imposed by the United States on cotton have probably benefited other cotton-exporting countries; her import restrictions on certain minerals and her import duty on wool have adverse effects on exporting countries, but they are not of great quantitative importance. A number of countries, especially in Western Europe, impose revenue duties on imports of such commodities as tea and coffee; they find this a convenient form of taxation, but the effect is to restrict their import demand for such commodities.[10] Restrictions on imports of manufactures affect at present only two or three underdeveloped countries, notably Hong Kong and India.

[10] See GATT, *Trends in International Trade; Report by a Panel of Experts* Geneva, 1958), pp. 103–10.

All this does not really amount to very much, and it must be remembered on the other side of the ledger that many underdeveloped countries consider it obviously right and proper to impose severe restrictions on imports of manufactured goods in order to promote their own industrialization. It may seem, therefore, that all the industrial countries can do is to avoid marked fluctuations in their economic activity resulting in sharp falls from time to time in their demand for imports. There are, however, two further possibilities which may be worth mentioning.

One possibility is to arrange, preferably through an international body, for long-term loans on easy terms to countries in balance-of-payments difficulties. The International Monetary Fund is designed to provide such loans (or, rather, an exchange of currencies) but only for a limited amount (depending on the size of the country's quota) and for periods of not more than three to five years.

Ideally, as I have urged earlier, a country should build up adequate reserves of foreign exchange when times are relatively good. But most underdeveloped countries need such public savings as they can make (through budget surpluses or Marketing Board profits) to invest in their own development, rather than to lock up in sterling or dollar balances. It might be helpful if such a country could set up a Development Corporation restricted to profit-earning enterprises (such as providing electric power)—other types of developmental projects (such as roads) could be paid for directly from the budget. Its Government would hold a substantial part of the shares in such a Development Corporation. The IMF (or some other international body) could undertake in advance to provide foreign exchange when needed on the security of such shares. The country would thus have a second line of defence against foreign-exchange shortages and could devote most of its savings to development.

Another possibility is available for primary products held by the United States stockpile. It would be expensive for underdeveloped countries to build up and maintain buffer stocks. But here is a stockpile already in existence, and although it was established on strategic grounds there is no reason why it should not serve a dual purpose. Suppose, to take rubber as an example, that the chief exporting and importing countries could agree on a reasonable price range (which might be varied from time to time) for RSS No 1 rubber (and differentials for other grades). The United States Government would simply announce that when the price went below the agreed floor it would buy at the floor price, and when the price went above the agreed ceiling it would sell at the ceiling price. If the price limits were fixed realistically, this would not cost the United States a cent. The mere knowledge that she would buy or sell when prices went outside these limits would prevent them from doing so; and all rubber-exporting countries would get what they say they want—a guarantee of relatively stable prices for their product.

CHAPTER IV

PRIVATE CAPITAL

THE FLOW OF PRIVATE CAPITAL

Several questions of definition arise in connexion with the flow of private capital into underdeveloped countries.

To begin with, private capital must be distinguished from public capital. This distinction is commonly made on the basis of whether the capital is provided by public authorities or by private investors, and not on the basis of who borrows and spends it. For example, a loan raised on the London (or any other) Stock Exchange by a Government is private capital, for it is subscribed by private investors. On the other hand, loans by the Export-Import Bank to private traders are public capital, for the capital of this bank is provided by the United States Government. Loans and investments by international organizations are classed as public. By far the most important of these is the World Bank, which obtains most of the capital it lends by selling its bonds to private investors.

Another question is whether the outflow of capital should be measured gross or net, that is to say whether reverse movements—flows of capital from the underdeveloped to the industrial countries—should be deducted. In the past there have been substantial repayments of external debt by the Governments of some underdeveloped countries. For example, the Government of India reduced its sterling debt, of some £400 million, to almost negligible proportions by 1945,[1] out of the sterling balances it acquired from the

[1] A. R. Conan, *Capital Imports into Sterling Countries* (London, Macmillan, 1960), p. 26.

United Kingdom's war expenditure in India. Again, the nominal value of United Kingdom investments in Latin America fell from £754 million in 1938 to £245 million in 1951,[2] owing to the repayment of government debt and the purchase of British-owned railways and other public utilities by Argentina and other countries with balances of foreign exchange accumulated during the war. Throughout the post-war period there have been sales of foreign-owned property (including shares) to local investors, and these continue. Increases in foreign-exchange holdings (such as sterling balances held by British colonies and ex-colonies) are short-term investments by the countries which own them. Except in connexion with balance-of-payments problems, we should perhaps consider gross rather than net outflow; the opening of a new oilfield or the establishment of a new factory by private foreign capital does not lose its importance because it is partly offset by sales of foreign-owned assets to local investors.

Again, there is the question of the re-investment or 'ploughing back' of undistributed profits by foreign-owned enterprises. The general view is that this should be included in the current outflow of private capital, although no transfer of foreign exchange is involved.

On the other hand, fortuitous changes in the 'book value' of assets owned by private foreign capital,[3] for example increases due to higher prices for the products and not to new investment or to re-investment of profits, should not be included in the outflow of capital.

A study issued by the Department of Economic and

[2] U.N. Dept. of Economic and Social Affairs, *Foreign Capital in Latin America* (N.Y., 1955), Table X, p. 156.
[3] The total of direct investment in all other countries was over $27 milliard for the United States in 1958 (*Survey of Current Business* (U.S. Dept. of Commerce), Aug. 1959, p. 30), and over £6,000 million for the United Kingdom (Conan, 'The UK as a Creditor Country', *Westminster Bank Review*, Aug. 1960), p. 17).

Social Affairs of the United Nations, *The International Flow of Private Capital 1956–1958*[4] divides private capital into long-term capital and medium or short-term capital. The latter consists largely of export credits; over a period, repayments tend to equal new lending. The study divides long-term capital into direct investments and portfolio investments. The distinction between the two is not always free from ambiguity.[5] Direct investment consists largely in the extension of a business through overseas branches or subsidiaries, while portfolio investments consist of Stock Exchange securities. However the essence of direct investment is that control is exercised by the foreign investors; and where this applies the investments are classed as direct (and not portfolio) investments, although the shares of the companies are Stock Exchange securities.

On this basis, the United Nations study points out that the bulk of the outflow of long-term private capital since the war has taken the form of direct investment. 'Since the end of the war entrepreneurial investments have accounted for the bulk of the international flow of private long-term capital, while investments in foreign bonds and shares were liquidated.'[6]

During recent years most of this flow has taken place between the more-developed countries themselves. Thus the outflow of private long-term capital from the United States (excluding retained profits of subsidiaries) in 1956, 1957, and 1958 respectively was 2,446, 2,694, and 2,090 million dollars, of which only 910, 1,449, and 844 million went to low-income countries (mainly Latin America).[7] Again, it was estimated in March 1960 that over the last seven years

[4] (N.Y., Dept. of Economic and Social Affairs, 1959).
[5] See Conan, *Capital Imports*, App. II for a discussion of this point.
[6] *International Flow of Private Capital*, p. 24.
[7] Ibid. p. 20.

United Kingdom private long-term investment overseas had averaged £300 million a year, of which 'something of the order of £100 million a year has been invested in less-developed areas.'[8] The United Nations study points out that 'the major development of the last few years is the growing capacity of Western Europe to export private capital', but adds that this 'will primarily result in greater capital movements among European countries themselves and between them and other high-income countries.'[9]

The reasons why private investors prefer more-developed countries are fairly obvious. They feel that their capital is more secure and that enterprises will be allowed more freedom than in most underdeveloped countries. Moreover the returns have been high, on the whole, during recent years; the average price-level of British equities doubled over the two years 1958–9 and there were marked rises on the stock exchanges of most industrial countries.

The consequence has been that the amount of external private long-term capital invested in underdeveloped countries has been comparatively small.

The region most favoured by private investors has been Latin America, which has been receiving well over a thousand million dollars a year. The *Economic Survey of Asia and the Far East 1959*[10] says (p. 86) that 'in the primary exporting countries of the region the net private capital inflow has been negligible in recent years, except in the Philippines and, to a lesser extent, in the Federation of Malaya and Singapore.' The Survey, however, is considering the net inflow, and deducting sales of property, shares, and other assets by overseas investors to local residents. It

[8] Cmnd. 974, para. 7.

[9] *International Flow of Private Capital*, p. 10.

[10] Published by the U.N. Economic Commission for Asia and the Far East (Bangkok, 1960).

seems also to omit the re-investment of undistributed profits, for instance in foreign-owned rubber and tea estates. Moreover its statistics only go up to 1957; in 1958 and 1959 India received a substantial inflow of private capital (including long-term credits), as well as public economic aid, to help her to complete her second five-year plan. My own view is that the gross inflow into this region has been and still is equivalent to several hundred million dollars a year.

The *Economic Survey of Africa since 1950*[11] points out (p. 222) that although 'on balance the gross inflow of foreign resources to most African countries was largely offset by an opposite flow', nevertheless 'the flow of external resources put at the disposal of African countries for investment has been considerable', 'it would seem that there has been a steady increase in the flow of foreign funds' and 'important development expenditures could not have taken place if foreign capital had not been available'.

Among the underdeveloped countries, it is those with oil resources which have attracted most foreign capital. A leading example is Venezuela. Some has been invested in other mineral development, for example copper in Northern Rhodesia and Chile and bauxite in Jamaica. Some has gone into manufacturing, but mainly in countries (such as Brazil and Mexico) which have already reached a certain level of development and have appreciable and expanding home markets. Once again we meet the rule that 'to him that hath shall be given'. The poorest countries, with few natural resources and relatively small home markets, continue to receive little private capital.

How large is the total gross outflow of private long-term capital (from non-Communist countries) to underdeveloped areas? The statistics are so inadequate that any estimate is

[11] Published by the U.N. Economic Commission for Africa (N.Y. 1959).

inevitably a very rough one. The United Nations estimate[12] is about 2 milliard dollars a year during 1955–8. But this excludes 'the profits which foreign enterprises re-invest in the underdeveloped countries where they operate'. If these are included, the total may be between $2\frac{1}{2}$ and 3 milliard dollars a year for recent years. The exact figure is of little importance. Whatever it is, it is certainly much less than the underdeveloped countries need.

THE SCOPE FOR DIRECT INVESTMENT

I pointed out earlier that the United Nations, rightly in my view, does not include private capital in economic aid. Nevertheless the inflow of private capital can make an important contribution to the economic growth of under-developed countries. This is especially true of direct investment.

Some of the chief industries, especially export industries, of underdeveloped countries have been built up largely by direct foreign investment. Leading examples are the oil industries of the Middle East and Venezuela; the rubber estates and tin mines of Malaya and Indonesia; the tea estates of India and Ceylon; the sugar estates of Cuba and the British West Indies; the banana estates of Central America; and the copper mines of Northern Rhodesia and Chile. In some countries, direct foreign investment has played a leading part also in the field of railways, electric power, and other public utilities, and in international trade.

While the inflow of capital in any form supplements the inadequate savings of low-income countries, direct investment has various advantages over loans (including export credits). Loans leave an aftermath of interest charges and repayments, which often become a serious burden on the budgets and foreign-exchange reserves of the borrowing

[12] *The International Flow of Private Capital*, p. 9.

countries. It is true that loans could be spent in ways which increase output, taxable capacity, and export earnings, but often they are not; they may be used for what seems an urgently-needed expansion of social services or to tide over a deficit in the balance of payments which turns out to be a long-period rather than a temporary deficit, so that the loans merely postpone the need to reduce levels of consumption. Direct investment leaves no such aftermath. The Government of the country incurs no obligation to make payments; if the industry goes through a lean period it is the foreign shareholders who suffer.[13]

Direct investment has other advantages also. It often introduces new industries or improved methods. It provides employment and sometimes specialized technical training for local workers. It contributes to local public revenue; for instance by paying income tax and in many cases export duties. If it establishes or expands export industries it increases exports and thereby foreign-exchange earnings. A number of large foreign companies (notably those owning estates) provide housing and social services for their workers.

Most underdeveloped countries, however, are very nationalistic. Against these advantages of foreign direct investment is the great disadvantage, from their standpoint, that it places control over part of their economic activity in the hands of foreigners. Some countries feel that large foreign companies may interfere in their political and economic life, introducing an element of foreign domination or, in the case of ex-colonies, re-introducing 'colonialism' through the back door. Moreover, most underdeveloped countries are socialistic in their outlook and consider that certain key industries, such as public utilities and steel

---

[13] The only problem which arises is that of providing foreign exchange against local currency to cover remittances home of profits (or repatriation of capital) by foreign companies or individuals.

mills, should be owned by the state rather than by private capital, whether foreign or local. Owing to these attitudes the scope for foreign direct investment has been substantially reduced since the war.

Public utilities, to begin with them, are an essential part of the 'infrastructure' required for economic development. In private hands their chief aim would be to make adequate profits. But Governments may consider, rightly or wrongly, that the national interests would be best served by a different policy. They may consider, for example, that services such as rail transport and the supply of electricity should be extended into relatively sparsely-populated areas, where the returns do not cover the costs. They may consider that the general level of charges should be kept low—too low to provide adequately for depreciation and also to yield a normal return on the capital. Even if the Government itself does not hold these views, it may be constrained to yield to general and local pressures to carry them out. Naturally private capital fights shy of making large fixed investments on these terms. As in any event most Governments want to own their public utilities, this is a field in which there now seems little scope for further private investment.[14]

Multi-purpose river-valley schemes and other large-scale projects to assist agriculture are nearly all owned and operated by Governments (or by public authorities under

[14] In Asia and Africa nearly all the public utilities are publicly owned. Argentina, Brazil, and Uruguay bought out foreign-owned railways and other public utilities in the early post-war years. Some two-thirds of the electricity-generating capacity in Latin America is still privately owned (mainly by foreign capital) but most of the new capacity is being constructed with public capital. 'Tariffs for electricity are far below overall price levels in Latin America . . . The discrepancy is so great in many Latin American countries that it has completely discouraged private investment and is a very heavy drain on public capital' (U.N. Economic Commission for Latin America, *Economic Survey of Latin America 1956* (N.Y. 1957), p. 111.

Governments). Such investments may yield a high return in increased output (although a number of them do not). This return could be transformed into a monetary yield by taxing the consequent increase in land values, but this can be done only by Governments. Before the war, some privately financed irrigation schemes paid good dividends, but nowadays many cultivators are reluctant to pay an adequate price for irrigation water even if it raises their incomes by considerably more. Private capital therefore tends to avoid such fields (except in so far as landowners can carry out smaller-scale measures on their own property), and to leave Governments the headache of trying to recover some revenue from their capital expenditure.

As I mentioned earlier, many of the large estates growing crops mainly for export are owned by foreign capital. Although they have a considerably larger output per worker than most neighbouring smallholdings, from time to time there are suggestions in some countries (for example, in Ceylon in connexion with tea estates)[15] that they should be nationalized and divided up into plots for local cultivators. So far, Governments (except in Indonesia and, recently, Cuba) have been deterred from taking this step by the high cost of fair compensation (and by the unfavourable consequences, including a severe check to any further inflow of any type of foreign capital into the country, which would result from confiscation) and perhaps also because they fear that such a change in ownership and management would lead to heavy falls in output and export earnings. But the danger of nationalization without fair compensation, however remote it may be, restricts the inflow of new foreign

[15] The Minister of Finance has declared that the new Government in Ceylon has no intention, now or later, of nationalizing estates (*The Times*, 25 July 1960). However, the seizing of American-owned sugar estates by the Cuban Government illustrates the danger.

capital into establishing new estates. Moreover, a number of countries would not be willing to alienate more land to foreign owners. Hence this important field is largely closed nowadays to foreign investment, although undistributed profits continue to be ploughed back into most of the present estates.

This leaves mainly mining, manufacturing, and trade as fields open to foreign direct investment. Even in these fields there are some limitations.

Most mining requires large investments and specialized technical knowledge and has therefore been left mainly to foreign capital.[16] Some countries, however, have a profound distrust of foreign oil companies, alleging that they tend to support whatever political parties or groups show them most favour. Mexico nationalized her oil industry in 1938 and in Iran the issue of nationalization virtually stopped the production of oil from 1951 to 1954.

In Argentina, which almost certainly has considerable reserves of oil in addition to those already being worked, there was for a long time very strong popular opposition to calling in foreign capital and enterprise to develop her oil. In 1958, however, she was importing 5–6 million tons a year—60 per cent. of her consumption—at a cost of $300 million a year, and she had very serious balance-of-payments deficits, both actual and prospective. President Frondizi felt compelled to call in foreign oil companies (partly on a basis of payment by results and in local currency) and the public of Argentina seems to have at last accepted this policy.

Brazil, however, which welcomes foreign capital in other fields, still refuses to admit foreign oil companies. (So do Chile and Uruguay.) Brazil is believed to have very sub-

---

[16] In some countries, however, notably India, mining is reserved for the state.

stantial deposits of oil, but so far her State Oilfields Administration (Petrobras) has not had marked success in its
prospecting, and the great bulk of the oil is still imported, at
a heavy cost in foreign exchange.

In the field of manufacturing, foreign capital is now welcomed in most countries, for they nearly all wish to become
more industrialized. Steel mills, however, are an exception.
A number of underdeveloped countries, at any rate in Asia
and Latin America, regard a steel mill as a symbol of
national prestige. But they want to have their own. They
may borrow to pay for it; they may employ foreign engineers to build it; but it (or they, for larger countries may have
more than one) must be government-owned. The same
applies, in some countries, to certain other large-scale enterprises such as oil refineries, chemical and fertilizer plants,
shipping lines, and air lines.

Foreign capital is not averse to entering the field of trade,
for as a rule this does not involve expensive fixed assets,
liable to confiscation. A number of countries, however, try
to reserve this field mainly for their own nationals and any
foreign companies already established may find themselves
discriminated against (for example, in the allotment of
government contracts or, where they are in force, of import
quotas).

MORE PRIVATE CAPITAL?

Are the underdeveloped countries likely to attract a substantially larger inflow of long-term foreign private capital?
If so, it will consist preponderantly of direct investment, as
it has done throughout the post-war years. Before discussing
how direct investment might be encouraged to expand, I
make some comments on private long-term loans to Governments and other public authorities in underdeveloped
countries.

'Underdeveloped countries account for only a small part of the limited foreign issues floated on the main capital markets since the end of the war.'[17] The total flow during recent years has probably been not much in excess of $100 million a year. It has consisted mainly of loans floated in London for the less-developed territories of the Commonwealth. Some loans have been floated also in New York (including loans for the Belgian Congo, Northern Rhodesia, Panama, and Jamaica).

There is a case for raising a loan for a specific revenue-producing project which will earn enough to cover interest and amortization charges. This is the type of loan made by the World Bank, and most loans subscribed to by private investors have conformed to this pattern.[18] Thus the White Paper of July 1957 on *The United Kingdom's Role in Commonwealth Development* (Cmnd. 237) says (para. 18):

> These loans are raised to finance public capital works undertaken by the Governments concerned or by public authorities. For example, the issue by the East African High Commission of £11·5 million in May of this year is to be used for the development of the railways, harbours, postal and telegraphic services in Africa.

Loans for general purposes, such as covering budget deficits or expanding social services, are in a different category. The great obstacle to them is that market rates of interest are so high. The private investor is not a philanthropist. He wants as high a return as he could get on other fixed-interest securities, such as those issued by the Governments or other public authorities of industrial countries, plus a risk-premium. He wants a risk-premium to guard against the danger that the borrowing Government may run into budgetary or balance-of-payments difficulties and be

---

[17] *The International Flow of Private Capital*, p. 66.
[18] The loans that have been raised by Israel on the New York market every year since 1951 are an exception. They are taken up by members of the American Jewish community, largely from non-economic motives.

compelled to default at least partially (as a number of such Governments did in the decade before the war), for instance by temporarily suspending interest payments or blocking their transfer. He also wants his interest and repayment to be in some international currency, such as dollars or sterling, in order to safeguard him against devaluation.

Today, yields approaching or exceeding 6 per cent. a year can be obtained from high-grade, fixed-interest securities in industrial countries. This means that underdeveloped countries would have to offer more. Why should they? The only economic justification for incurring these heavy interest burdens is that a country expects to make such rapid economic progress, over the period of the loan, that it will be able to repay the principal with comparative ease when the time comes. Very few underdeveloped countries have such favourable prospects. If they nevertheless do float loans at rates of interest high enough to attract private investors, they are either deluding themselves and possibly sowing the seeds of a severe economic setback in the future, or else they are hoping, consciously or unconsciously, that when the time comes for repayment somebody will come to their rescue.[19]

The establishment of institutions such as the World Bank or the Commonwealth Development Finance Company does not overcome the obstacle of high interest charges. Such institutions may play a valuable part in assessing the prospects of different projects and in giving technical

[19] If the borrowing country begins making annual payments, almost at once, into a sinking fund, the burden of repayment is spread over the life of the loan, and no crisis will arise when the loan matures. In my view, however, a country which expects to make rapid economic progress is fully justified in investing all the capital at its disposal in developmental projects, provided that such projects yield a return (in terms of increased output, if not of money revenue) substantially higher than the yield which would be obtained by purchasing securities for sinking funds.

assistance. The private investor feels that he has better security, and is therefore willing to lend for less, when he lends to such an institution. But he still expects to receive the market rate of interest and the charges to the borrowing country are still high. The conclusion remains valid that it does not pay most underdeveloped countries to float long-term loans, except for specific revenue-producing projects.

The Government of a country with an ambitious development plan but limited taxable capacity may look hopefully at the possibility of floating a long-term loan to bridge the gap between its aspirations and its resources. But it will not get loans on easy terms, with low rates of interest and with repayments spread over a long period and preferably in its own currency, from private investors or from institutions such as the World Bank. Such loans will be provided only as a form of economic aid by Governments which, for political or other reasons, wish to help the borrowing country, or by an international institution established for that purpose, such as the International Development Association.

I turn to direct investment. Owing to the burden of interest charges on loans, direct investment has formed over 90 per cent. of the inflow of long-term private capital into underdeveloped countries since the war and will probably continue to do so. Nevertheless it amounts to less than 2 per cent. of the combined national incomes of underdeveloped countries and is concentrated largely in a small number of them, notably those exporting oil.

A substantial expansion of the flow of direct investment might be encouraged by the discovery of new investment opportunities; by a more liberal attitude by underdeveloped countries as to the fields within which private capital is permitted; and above all by a change in the climate of opinion towards foreign capital, perhaps supported by some arrangements and guarantees, which would give private foreign investors more confidence.

A number of countries have embarked on development plans with only a hazy notion of the extent of their natural resources and production possibilities. A few examples will illustrate the kinds of new investment opportunities to which I refer. Very large deposits of oil have been found in Libya and other deposits elsewhere, for example in the Sahara and (to a limited extent) in India; rich deposits of bauxite were found in Jamaica during the war and others, more recently, of iron ore in Venezuela; coffee-growing has expanded greatly in some African countries and there are clearly potentialities for the expansion of other crops, such as rice, in parts of Africa; Peru and Chile have recently developed a large and growing output of fish-meal; the application of a new process in 1954 raised Mexico's output of sulphur from a few thousand tons to over a million a year.

There is no doubt that many possibilities of this kind would be revealed by fuller investigation: geological surveys; experiments with new crops, new methods, new processes; pilot plants; and so forth. In my view underdeveloped countries should give high priority to this kind of research and experiment, whether financed from external aid or from their own resources. A number of bodies, including the Colonial Development Corporation, have been engaged partly on this type of work, but their funds are very inadequate. The most important of them all, the United Nations Special Fund, set up at the beginning of 1959 for this express purpose, approved 44 projects costing $75 million in its first year (of which hardly any has yet been spent) and seems unlikely to be able to raise this figure above, say, $200 million a year for some time to come.[20]

[20] The Fund obtains its revenue solely from voluntary annual contributions (varying in amount from year to year) by member Govern-

[*Continued on next page*

I showed in the preceding section that in most underdeveloped countries the fields open to private capital are
much more restricted than before the war. I think it would
be realistic and sensible for some of them to revise their
present attitude on this question, at any rate for the next
few years. Whatever the theoretical merits of public enterprise, most of these countries have at present relatively few
civil servants trained and qualified to run state enterprises.
If more enterprises and activities could be left to private
capital, this would free their senior civil servants for other
urgent and important tasks. (This is doubtless a major
reason why the Central Government of India has now given
up control of trade in staple foodstuffs, involving the
enforcement of price-fixing and other regulations.) These
countries are also very short of capital, so that if foreign
capital could be induced to enter such fields their own
limited capital would be available for other purposes.

One of these fields is that of public utilities. It would not
be impossible to attract foreign capital into this field. For
example, a foreign company could be guaranteed a certain
minimum level of profits. In general, this is not a good policy:
private enterprise should be prepared to risk making losses,
and guaranteed profits reduce incentives to efficiency. However, in this particular field, where large amounts of fixed
capital are required and where the state would probably

---

ments of the United Nations. It requires recipient countries to contribute
to projects carried out for their benefit. Thus the $75 million approved
in its first year was made up of $31 million in contributions from member
Governments and $44 million from recipient countries. Projects will be
carried out by United Nations agencies (such as the FAO). At present,
the activities of the Fund 'are wholly devoted to the financing of resource
surveys, applied research and vocational and advanced technical
training'. It is 'concentrating on relatively large projects which will open
doors to fruitful investment'. See '*One Hundred Countries, One and One
Quarter Billion People*' by Paul G. Hoffman, pp. 39–43, which lists the
forty-four projects mentioned above. Mr Hoffman is the Director of
the Fund.

control the charges and the general policy of a private company, some such guarantee is needed. Thus in 1953 the Mexican Government agreed to rates being charged by a United States company (the Mexican Light and Power Company Ltd.) which would give an annual net return of 8 per cent.—after Mexican taxes—on the assessed value of the investment.[21]

Again, more foreign capital might be attracted into estates if Governments were willing to alienate land for this purpose and to promise not to nationalize such estates for a stated period, and thereafter to nationalize them (if at all) only subject to compensation to be assessed by a named international body. Some Governments, anxious to attract foreign capital and expertise, might go further and give guarantees for a period against arbitrary increases in taxes such as export duties (which, however, might be on a fixed sliding-scale).

On similar terms, more foreign capital might be attracted into mining; and countries such as India which reserve mining for the state might throw it open, at least partly, to private enterprise.

I mentioned earlier that certain large-scale enterprises, such as steel mills and air lines, are commonly reserved for the state. This is a considerable drain on the limited amount of local capital and administrative ability. Indonesia would be in a better position today had she come to an agreement with the Dutch under which they continued to operate their KPM fleet; and India would not be so desperately short of capital had she accepted offers such as that made by the West German firms to take over the steel mill they are building. But nationalism, perhaps the greatest curse of our age, nearly always prevails over economic considerations.

[21] U.N. Dept. of Economic and Social Affairs, *Foreign Capital in Latin America*, p. 13 n.

A marked expansion of foreign direct investment, whether in fields still open to it or in fields at present reserved for public enterprise, depends above all else on a favourable attitude by the capital-receiving countries. There is nothing, say the Americans, so timid as a million dollars. The potential foreign investor is haunted by all kinds of fears. He fears that his assets may be confiscated, or nationalized without fair compensation. He fears that he may be compelled to employ too high a proportion of local people, even if they lack the necessary qualifications, on his senior staff. He fears that he may be subjected to various regulations which make it difficult or impossible for him to operate at a profit. He fears that discriminatory taxation may be imposed on his enterprise. He fears that he may not be allowed to repatriate any of his capital or to remit home his profits (or more than a very limited amount) and that he may be compelled to reinvest all or most of his undistributed profits in the country. All these blows have fallen on foreign capital in certain countries at certain times, and he fears that they may fall again.[22]

What can be done to give potential foreign investors more confidence? It has been suggested from time to time[23] that a World Investment Code should be drawn up and signed by investing and receiving countries in order to provide agreed safeguards for both. The Code might have a secretariat to administer it and an arbitration tribunal to deal with disputes. This proposal is discussed in the pamphlet *A World Investment Convention?* published in July 1959 by

[22] This is not to deny that foreign companies should sympathize with the needs and aspirations of underdeveloped countries and should give them (as indeed most foreign companies do) whatever assistance they can reasonably be expected to give, e.g. in training local people for senior posts, in providing the Government with technical advice when requested, and in conforming as far as they can to the general economic policies of the country.

[23] For instance in the United Nations, in the Council of Europe, and by statesmen such as the Prime Minister of the Federation of Malaya.

the Parliamentary Group for World Government (House of Commons, London).

Whether it will be possible for such a Code to be drawn up and accepted in the near future is perhaps doubtful. But there are various measures which countries could take unilaterally. A country eager to attract foreign capital could give various undertakings (as Mr. Nehru undertook not to nationalize foreign enterprises for at least ten years), perhaps supported by an offer to submit to international arbitration if foreign capital claimed that such undertakings had been broken. It would be unduly pessimistic to dismiss such undertakings as worthless on the ground that they might be repudiated if there were a change of Government. National pride has its advantages as well as its disadvantages, and few Governments would feel happy at repudiating formal guarantees given by their predecessors. There is also the important point that such a breach of faith would dry up the flow of further foreign capital, which would probably still be badly needed.

. . . The Governments of most capital-exporting countries now insure export credits under comprehensive schemes. The risks covered are usually insolvency of the foreign buyer or failure to pay within a reasonable time after due date for goods accepted; war or revolution; transfer delays and other risks occurring outside the exporter's country and beyond the control of both the exporter and buyer.[24]

Could not capital-exporting countries, either individually or (preferably) acting in concert through a joint institution, operate a similar scheme for long-term investment? Among the risks covered could be the risk of confiscation, or nationalization without fair compensation, and restrictions on the remittance home of profits.[25] A few underdeveloped

[24] *The International Flow of Private Capital 1956–1958,* p. 70.
[25] The United States Government, through its Investment Guaranty Programme, has provided insurance against these and similar risks since 1958 for new investment in countries whose Governments have agreed to participate in the scheme.

countries might have to be excluded, on the grounds that
their economic and financial policies made the risks too
great, and the premiums might have to vary somewhat
among countries, but I can see no insuperable objection to
such a scheme. Possibly the Governments of the capital-
exporting countries might give a subsidy in order to keep
the premiums fairly low; this would be a valuable form of
economic aid.

Another way in which capital-exporting countries could
help is by tax concessions. Most of them do have arrangements which prevent double taxation. They might go
further, and provide that their companies operating abroad
are not taxed more heavily than local companies in the
same country.[26]

There are various devices which some underdeveloped
countries have adopted, and others might adopt, in order to
attract foreign direct investment. One such device is for the
Government of the country to associate itself as a partner
with one or more foreign firms, thus giving them more
confidence that they will be permitted to make reasonable
profits and will not be discriminated against. Thus the
Government of Burma has established a number of such
'joint ventures', the most important being that with the
Burmah Oil Company. A similar device is for the Government to hold shares in some type of Development Corporation in which foreign capital is encouraged to participate.
The Industrial Credit and Investment Corporation of
India, for instance, set up at the beginning of 1955, was
sponsored by a 'group of private interests in India, the

[26] The United Kingdom went some considerable distance in this
direction in the Finance Act of 1957. Concerns that qualify as 'oversea
trade corporations' are exempted from United Kingdom income tax
and profits tax on their trading profits earned abroad. But dividends
remitted back to United Kingdom shareholders are subject to United
Kingdom income tax, so that United Kingdom shareholders do not
benefit fully from local 'tax holidays.'

United Kingdom and the United States and is assisted by the Government of India and the IBRD'.[27] Its purpose is to stimulate 'industrial expansion in the private sector'. So far it has authorized the expenditure of between £1 and £2 million, has given financial assistance to various firms, and has set up a number of new ones (all mainly in manufacturing).[28]

The most common method of attracting direct foreign investment has been to impose tariffs or other restrictions on imports. This has induced foreign companies making products (for example, cigarettes or soap) with an established market (and marketing organization) in the country to set up local branches or subsidiaries in order to protect their market. The Government often gives an explicit or implied undertaking that restrictions on imports will continue, and that new competing firms will not be permitted, so long as the plants thus established inside the import barriers are working below full capacity.

Whether or not protection for local manufactures stimulates economic growth may depend on circumstances. Personally I believe that in most countries it leads to a waste of resources. But, however this may be, it is clear that protection, and the expectation that it will continue, is a means of attracting foreign capital.

[27] *Institutions for Industrial Finance and Development*, Lok Sabha Secretariat, New Delhi. July 1955, pp. 10–12.

[28] The International Finance Corporation should be mentioned. It is separate from, but closely affiliated with, the World Bank. It has an authorized capital of $100 million, of which $93 million, subscribed by fifty-seven Governments, has been paid up. Its purpose is to encourage 'productive and profitable' private investment, mainly in less-developed countries, in industrial enterprises. It normally expects private investors (local or foreign) to put up at least half the capital; it does not require a government guarantee of repayment; and it hopes to revolve its funds by selling its holdings to private investors when the enterprise is successfully established. It was set up in 1956, but by September 1958 it had committed itself to investments of little more than $10 million, nearly half in Brazil.

A major argument often put forward in favour of protection is that it attracts 'infant industries' which will later (perhaps with the help of external economies provided by other infant industries) be able to stand on their own feet. In my view, a better way of attracting such industries would be to give them an annual subsidy from public revenue or to rely on special tax concessions such as a 'tax holiday' (freedom from income-tax) for the first five years or more.

In some industries a large-scale plant is by far the most efficient. But the home market of a number of countries is too small for such a plant to work to anything approaching full capacity, and there is no prospect of exports. A possible solution, in some cases, is for a number of such countries to form a common market large enough to absorb the output of such a plant; one of the countries could have a plant producing one product (for example, cement), another a plant producing a different product (for example, paper), and so on. Such a scheme is proposed for the five Central American republics of Costa Rica, El Salvador, Guatemala, Honduras, and Nicaragua.

In a number of countries, a general reform which would make them more attractive to private capital would be the abolition of various forms of control, especially exchange control. This view has been strongly expressed by the Chairman of the Chartered Bank, Mr. V. A. Grantham. 'Their inexperienced politicians and civil servants', he said, 'often find it beyond their power to run restricted and controlled economies'. What they need is 'a control-free administration which would eliminate opportunities for bribery and corruption and a unit of currency having the same internal and external value, thus eliminating the rewards of smuggling and other forms of currency evasion which run down the country's external assets'.[29]

[29] *Report of the Directors of The Chartered Bank 1960*, p. 40.

The most important factor affecting the flow of foreign capital for direct investment is the attitude towards it of the underdeveloped countries. It is too early to form a judgement about the majority of African countries which have recently gained, or soon will gain, their independence. For nearly all countries in Latin America, however, and for most countries in Asia, there are good grounds for believing that today they welcome foreign capital and are trying to encourage it.

In the early post-war years, a number of them adopted a different attitude. They were under the illusion that foreign private capital was very anxious to come in, but they were not prepared to admit it freely. They therefore decided to allow foreign capital only in certain approved industries and subject to various conditions and regulations. As time went on, they discovered that comparatively little foreign capital (except in oil) was attracted on these terms. They came to realize that although the primary aim of capital is to make profits, foreign direct investment might pay an important and useful part in their economies. Their attitude has therefore changed. The Government of India, for instance, has stopped enforcing its rules about majority control and ownership by Indians and has opened up to private enterprise some fields formerly reserved for the state. Again, in most Latin American countries the remittance home of profits is now virtually unrestricted. A number of countries have introduced 'tax holidays'.[30] Although many underdeveloped countries remain fundamentally socialistic in their outlook, they seem to be coming round to the view that fewer 'controls' and a more welcoming attitude to

---

[30] But usually combined with restrictions on competing imports. For details of tax holidays and similar tax incentives in force in particular underdeveloped countries see International Chamber of Commerce, *Taxation and the Developing Nations* (Paris, 1959).

foreign capital and private enterprise may help to accelerate their economic growth.[31]

[31] The following passage from the U.N. *Economic Bulletin for Asia and the Far East*, vol. viii, no. 1, May 1957 is quoted by Conan, *op cit.* p. 96.

'There is no doubt that in certain respects new regulations that have grown up since 1905 have made investment in the region [Asia and the Far East] less attractive to foreign investors than before. For example, the fields in which it can operate have been somewhat curtailed on the whole, the degree of required participation of local capital, management and labour has been increased in many countries and repatriation of income and capital has in some cases been made less free.'

Admittedly it is difficult to generalize, and attitudes vary from one country to another. Nevertheless I consider that this quotation is very misleading. It may apply to two or three countries, such as Indonesia, but most countries nowadays welcome foreign capital and have relaxed their restrictions on it.

CHAPTER V

THE FUTURE OF ECONOMIC AID

MOTIVES FOR PROVIDING ECONOMIC AID

THE motive which statesmen and others in the aid-giving countries nearly always place first is the moral duty of the richer countries to help the poorer. We are all fellow human beings living together in the same world, yet there is an enormous gulf between standards of living, even of the lowest-paid workers, in the more advanced and in the least-developed countries. In the latter the mass of the people are poorly fed, clothed, and housed. Many of them suffer from disease or ill-health. A high proportion cannot read or write. Most of them have never travelled more than a few miles from where they live. They lack nearly all the comforts and amenities of Western civilization. They cannot develop their talents and potentialities or enjoy anything approaching a full life. The gulf is so great that it deeply shocks all who realize it. It is our plain duty to make a sincere, substantial, and sustained effort to diminish it.

This, after all, is what we do within our own countries. The poorer members of the national community are assured of a reasonable minimum standard of living, including education, health, and other social services. This is done compulsorily, through the machinery of public finance (including national insurance and grants-in-aid to the poorer areas), because we recognize that voluntary efforts alone would be inadequate and would enable the more selfish to escape their fair share of the necessary contributions. In the name of our common humanity, why not apply the same principles of economic aid to the less-developed regions of the world?

Personally I find this argument entirely convincing and I fully accept its consequences. My only proviso is that we should make sure that our aid achieves its purpose and does not go down the drain of corruption and incompetence. While I do not doubt the sincerity of those public figures who stress our moral duty, the record shows that other considerations have been more dominant. The very inadequate amount of economic aid which legislators have been persuaded to provide has not gone where it was most needed. Its distribution has been governed largely by the political and economic policies of the chief aid-giving countries. I discuss below two aims which have played a leading part. One is to use economic aid as a 'cold-war' weapon, or prophylactic, against Communism. The other is to use it as a means of promoting trade, especially exports from the industrial countries.

ECONOMIC AID AS A WEAPON AGAINST COMMUNISM

There is a widespread belief that unless the West provides substantial assistance to help certain underdeveloped countries to raise their standards of living they are likely to turn to Communism. A phrase such as 'turning to Communism' covers a number of different possibilities. It may mean that a party labelled 'Communist' wins the elections and comes into power. In that event it might enter into close political, military, and economic relations with the Soviet Union, becoming part of the Soviet bloc. This need not happen. Marshal Tito follows an independent course and so, I think, does Ho Chi Minh, although less obviously. The Soviet Union and China have their differences. I doubt whether countries such as, say, Indonesia, Iraq, Guinea, or Cuba would become 'puppets of Moscow' should they turn

Communist. Suppose, however, that every country which turns Communist enters fully into the Soviet orbit. What of it? In this age of inter-continental missiles, with the Soviet Union and the United States the only two nuclear powers of real importance, I cannot see that it would be of much military significance if a number of countries in Asia, Africa, and even Latin America joined the Soviet bloc. They would not be countries of much military strength; they could hardly affect the outcome of a nuclear war.

But I am no expert on this subject and I may be quite wrong. There may be considerations of infiltration, espionage, local wars with conventional forces, and so forth, which would give the West grounds for serious alarm at the emergence of a number of new Communist countries. However this may be, if the West wishes to prevent a particular country from going Communist, the appropriate weapon is seldom economic aid. Countries have their national pride; they are not going to be bribed by a few dollars a year per head of population into following political or economic policies of which the West approves, if they believe that a different course would be in their best interests. If a country wishes to remain independent and is confronted with a Communist neighbour which might conquer and absorb it, its only defence is military strength. On these grounds the United States provides military aid to South Korea, South Vietnam, and Taiwan; the economic aid which she also provides to them may be regarded as a supplement.

It is not true that poverty breeds Communism. Before the war Communism was very weak in the relatively poor countries of Eastern Europe; the only influential Communist Party was in relatively prosperous Czechoslovakia. Today, the strongest Communist parties in Western Europe are in France and Italy, and they draw their support mainly from the industrial areas, rather than from the poorer rural areas. India made some economic progress from 1952 to 1957, and the Communist vote grew from 4 million to 12 million. If any generalization on this subject is valid, it is that in a poor country the growth of education and industrialization is likely to lead to discontent and a search for ways of speeding up economic growth; a soil in which the seeds of Communist propaganda may thrive.

Another possible meaning of 'turning to Communism' is that a country may follow economic policies commonly associated with Communism, such as compulsory saving, public rather than private enterprise, and collective farms. But it may follow such policies without having a Communist Government or, even if it has, without associating itself with the Soviet bloc. The relevant question here is whether a particular policy is the most suitable for the country in question. Most underdeveloped countries need to save more in order to increase their own capital and to speed up their development, at the cost of keeping their standards of living lower for the time being than they might be. A number of non-Communist countries follow this course; for example, India has recently increased her taxation and Ghana and Burma have built up substantial surpluses through their Marketing Boards.

I believe, as I urged in the last chapter, that many underdeveloped countries would be well advised to give more scope to private enterprise. But in some countries there may be a lack of entrepreneurs and a shortage of private capital, so that unless the Government take the initiative little will be done.[1] Turkey, for example, is an anti-Communist country, but in Turkey most of the larger enterprises are owned and run by public authorities. In the same way, as I

[1] This point of view is forcibly argued, with illustrations, by A. H. Hanson, *Public Enterprise and Economic Development* (London 1959).

have argued earlier, there may be a case in some under-developed areas for something resembling collective farms, on the lines of the Gezira scheme in the Sudan.

The really shocking aspect of life in Communist countries is the suppression of basic human liberties. It is a scandal that the United States has allowed two or three countries which she has taken under her wing, for example South Korea until President Rhee was thrown out in June 1960, to be police states. I would make it a condition of aid that the receiving countries should permit freedom of speech, discussion, worship, and travel, should not allow punish-ment without fair trial, should permit citizens to read foreign publications and listen to foreign broadcasts. I realise that a dogmatic insistence on all aspects of this con-dition would not be practicable, for various reasons, in certain countries; but I think that the condition should be laid down as a general principle.

Another possible meaning of 'turning to Communism' is accepting Soviet aid. I have indicated in Chapter II that the extent of Soviet aid is often greatly exaggerated.[2] But surely the West should welcome Soviet aid and should try to in-fluence the Soviet countries to give more (at the same time suggesting that Soviet aid should be co-ordinated with their own, in order to prevent duplication and overlapping). The underdeveloped countries need all the aid they can get, from whatever source. A secondary consideration, if we think in terms of the cold war, is that the more aid Soviet countries provide the slower will be their own economic growth. (And

---

[2] This exaggeration continues. For example, Guinea is commonly said to be crowded with Soviet 'technicians'. The *Economist* (25 June 1960, p. 1346) points out that: 'Against perhaps 3,000 French and Western technicians and administrators in Guinea, the whole Communist Bloc (which works as a team) has rarely more than 150 personnel at a time—though the planes arrive almost daily bringing new ones and taking others away.'

therefore they are not likely to provide a great deal. To indulge for a moment in fantasy, if the Soviet Union made herself responsible for the economic growth of another ten or more countries, we should soon hear some bitter recriminations from them about the inadequacy of her help.)

The strongest weapon against Communism (except where military strength is appropriate) is intelligent propaganda, stressing, for example, the suppression of personal freedom in Communist countries, the events of the revolution in Hungary, the desperate efforts of refugees to leave East Germany for West Germany, North Vietnam for South Vietnam, China for Hong Kong. The worst possible kind of propaganda is to make a bogey of 'Communism' and to make a case for economic aid (as the United States Government does every year to Congress) on the ground that otherwise countries may 'turn Communist'. For this implies that the 'ideological conflict' is of paramount importance. It implies that the only alternative to a free-enterprise society on modern lines is to adopt Communism, lock, stock, and barrel. This of course is not true; there is a wide variety of different arrangements suited to the circumstances of particular countries. The idea that 'Communism' is the devil, one and indivisible and everywhere the same, merely plays into the hands of Soviet propaganda.[3]

ECONOMIC AID AS A MEANS OF PROMOTING TRADE

Nowadays the industrial countries have no difficulty in finding sources of supply for raw materials and other imports but most of them would like to earn more foreign exchange by expanding their exports. An argument for

[3] For an excellent statement of this view, see the thoughtful lecture by Eugene R. Black, 'The Age of Economic Development,' *Economic Journal*, June 1960, pp. 274–5.

economic aid which often carries considerable weight in an aid-giving country is that it will lead to an expansion of its exports. This argument seems obviously valid for export credits provided by the Government of an industrial country (or by the exporting firms themselves) which are tied to specific exports from that country. However, if we consider all the industrial countries together, export credits will bring about an expansion of their combined exports only if the underdeveloped countries are thereby induced to import more than they otherwise would (or enabled to import more than they otherwise could). If this were not so, the consequence would be merely a switching of their purchases away from some industrial countries towards others which gave more generous credit.

As a rule, export credits, by giving the purchasing countries time to pay, do lead to an expansion of their imports. But this may be a mixed blessing. After a time it may become clear that a country has been over-importing and is in serious balance-of-payments difficulties. It may have to raise stabilization loans (saddling it with the burden of interest and repayment charges) to keep it on its feet and, incidentally, to bail out the over-zealous exporting firms in the industrial countries. (This has happened during recent years in, for example, several Latin American countries.) Moreover it may be constrained (depending partly on the movements in its terms of trade) to restrict its imports in order to pay off its debts.

There seems to be a case for the industrial countries setting up a joint organization to provide export credits. This would prevent them from competing with one another as to the terms on which they provided credit (although of course they would still compete in price, quality, delivery dates, and so forth); it would help both them and the purchasing countries by keeping the amount of credit given to any country within its capacity to pay, thus avoiding over-importing; and it would leave a purchasing country free to buy—on credit—from whatever source could offer it the best value for the types of goods which it considered most suitable.

Export credits, at market rates of interest, are not, strictly, economic aid. Outright grants, or loans on easy terms, by the Government of an industrial country are sometimes tied to specific exports from that country. This may considerably diminish the value of the aid. If the goods are given freely, the receiving country may merely note with amused tolerance that the donor country has put a (nominal) price on them well above the prices at which some other country is selling similar goods. But if the goods are, for example, items of plant and equipment with which local engineers and technicians are unfamiliar and which they consider unsuitable for local requirements, the gift may lead to friction. By far the most satisfactory course is for a donor country to give money (or its equivalent, for example, commodities such as wheat which can be readily sold) and to leave the underdeveloped countries free to import whatever types of capital equipment and so forth they consider most suitable and from whatever sources they think offer them the best value.

It is true that aid tied to particular exports does enable a donor Government to reply to the query 'What do *we* get out of it?' by citing those exports. This is not really much of an answer in the case of an outright grant, for the exports will never be paid for, and nowadays a country can maintain full employment without giving exports away. (This is doubtless one reason why the United States is considering switching her aid to loans rather than grants.) However it is an answer which may satisfy the many people who hold the curious belief that exports are somehow good in themselves rather than merely a means to obtain foreign exchange.[4]

It is true that economic aid, even if not tied to any exports, will speed up the economic growth of under-developed countries and may thereby lead eventually to a continuous expansion of international trade from which all countries will benefit, and those which rely heavily on exports will benefit most. But this is a very long-term prospect. The rate of economic growth of most underdeveloped countries is so slow that it will take a long time, on present form, before they increase their imports from industrial countries very substantially, and meanwhile many of them are attempting to make themselves more self-sufficient by substituting locally produced goods for imported ones. However it must be remembered that the industrial countries trade mainly with one another. As the under-developed countries become less poor their international trade is likely to grow, even if at the same time they become more industrialized. So far as it goes, this is an argument—addressed to the self-interest of industrial countries—for a substantial increase in the amount of their economic aid.

In the short run, however, they should not expect too much. Economic aid involves a real sacrifice. It is misleading to urge that it will pay for itself in increased exports. A shop-keeper who gave, say, £10 a year to every family in his street might justifiably conclude that some of it would be spent in his shop. Even so he would recover only the profit—say 20 per cent.—on his increased turnover. The rest would be a sheer loss.

Similarly with an industrial country. There are plenty of ways in which money could be invested at home—better

[4] In some cases there is a little more than this to the argument. The export of some capital goods may lead to a future stream of orders for spare parts and replacements and the export of some consumer goods may help to create a taste or preference for them.

roads, improved hospitals, slum clearance and housing, for example—which would provide employment and raise standards of living. If the money is given instead to under-developed countries, the donor country will get much less benefit. But the purpose of economic aid is to help the under-developed countries, not to perform a sleight-of-hand by which the wealthier countries are providing 'economic aid' at no real cost to themselves.

ARGUMENTS AGAINST ECONOMIC AID

One argument sometimes put forward against providing economic aid to certain countries is that they are not really grateful for it. They do not like the white man, even when he bears gifts; and should the opportunity arise, they would be quite prepared, metaphorically if not indeed literally, to stab him in the back. Why, then, should we help them?

It is very human to resent having to accept assistance, even when it is badly needed; and we should not expect to buy friendship with money. In order to gain the goodwill and co-operation of the underdeveloped countries with whom we share this ever-shrinking world we must genuinely put their needs and interests first in the amount and type of aid which we provide and in the manner in which we provide it; we must respect their national pride and avoid any semblance of patronage, superiority, and racial discrimination. As time goes on, aid provided in this spirit will, we hope, gradually dispel bitterness and hostility, where they exist.

Another argument against aid is to ask, with illustrations, 'Why should we help them when they make so little effort to help themselves?' Why, for example, should workers in industrial countries who have a 40 to 48 hour working week make sacrifices for countries where the majority of the workers work little more than 20 hours a week, and not very hard at that? Why should a country which taxes itself 30 or 35 per cent. of its national income give aid to countries which tax themselves much more lightly, many of them less than 10 per cent. of their national incomes?

It is just because most underdeveloped countries are so poor that their workers lack health and vigour and earn too little to overcome their preference for leisure, especially in a hot climate. It is just because they are so poor that they have such a narrow margin of taxable capacity. A number of them are struggling to help themselves—for example by community development schemes and more effective measures of assessing and collecting taxes—but their great problem is their poverty and the 'vicious circles' arising from it.

A view perhaps worth mentioning is that economic aid may teach a country to become less self-reliant and to slacken its own efforts to improve its conditions. There might be some force in this view if aid were on a massive scale and consisted largely of consumer goods but (except possibly in one or two countries, such as Laos) the actual situation is nothing like that. Economic aid is on a relatively small scale and consists mainly of aid for projects of capital formation. The three or four million tons of wheat a year which the United States is giving to India over the next four years (to take a leading example of aid in the form of consumer goods) will not retard any efforts which India would otherwise make to improve her agriculture, for her consumption of food grains is over 70 million tons a year. The maximum probable increase in economic aid to most underdeveloped countries is very unlikely to be a substitute for self-help; and in any event nearly all such countries have development plans which depend mainly on their own efforts and resources, to which external aid is only a supplement.

Professor Milton Friedman has urged[5] that all economic aid should be stopped, on the ground that

in the long run it will almost surely retard economic development and promote the triumph of Communism.

The Pharaohs raised enormous sums of capital to build the pyramids; this was capital formation on a grand scale; it certainly did not promote economic development in the fundamental sense of contributing to a self-sustaining growth in the standard of life of the Egyptian masses. Modern Egypt has under government auspices built a steel mill; but it is a drain on the economic resources of Egypt, not a contribution to its economic strength, since the cost of making steel in Egypt is very much greater than the cost of buying it elsewhere; it is simply a modern equivalent of the pyramids except that maintenance expenses are higher.

Professor Friedman considers that such 'modern monuments' are 'almost certain to be the rule'. He objects to 'a centralized program of economic development' which (in contrast to 'a vigorous, free, capitalistic market') introduces rigidity and inflexibility. Such centralized programmes, with their state enterprises, are, he thinks, 'a threat to the preservation of a free world' and will speed up 'communization' in underdeveloped countries.

I agree that in some countries, although not in all, such state enterprises as steel mills and air lines involve a waste of resources. But if countries are determined to have them, either as symbols of national prestige or because they believe that such enterprises in fact help, rather than hinder, economic growth, I do not find this a convincing reason for refusing them economic aid. They will go ahead with such projects, whether they get economic aid or not, and if the consequence is to make them still poorer their need for aid becomes still greater. We might as logically refuse aid to a country because its religious beliefs involve some economic

[5] 'Foreign Economic Aid: Means and Objectives'. *Yale Review*, June 1958, vol. xlvii, no. 4.

sacrifice, declaring that building pagodas in Burma is a waste of capital or that the sacred cows of India are an economic liability.

If the development programme of a country consisted almost entirely of projects that were clearly wasteful, we might refuse to assist it in its folly. But that is not the case. With due respect to Professor Friedman, 'modern monuments' are very far from being 'the rule'. By far the greater part of most development programmes consists of improvements to agricultural land or to means of transport and communication, expanded supplies of electric power, and other measures (including expenditure on health, education, and housing) which obviously tend to raise output and standards of living.

I agree that some underdeveloped countries might do better with less government control. But the pattern of American economic life is not necessarily the most suitable for every country, and it seems to me quite unjustified to raise the bogey of 'Communism' and to refuse economic aid to a country in which public enterprise plays a relatively large part.

Professor P. T. Bauer has written a book on *United States Aid and Indian Economic Development*.[6] His general objection to Indian planning is the same as that of Professor Friedman to planning in most underdeveloped countries. It places far too much control in the hands of the central Government and other public authorities; it restricts and hampers private enterprise; it leads to a regimented and probably, eventually, a totalitarian society. He also criticizes various policies embodied in the plans. One of his major criticisms is of the massive expenditure on heavy industry, especially on steel plants.

---

[6] (Washington D.C., American Enterprise Association, 1959).

While it is true that in most countries the path to healthy industrialization lies through increasing output per worker in agriculture, I cannot agree that steel plants in India involve a waste of capital. It is quite wrong to place the steel industries of India in the same category as those of some other underdeveloped countries, which lack the raw materials for steel production. India has large reserves of rich iron ore and adequate reserves of fairly good coking coal. The efficiency of Indian steel workers will improve with training, and wages are relatively low. India can therefore produce steel at a comparatively low cost, and if all the increased output cannot be sold locally, some of it can be exported.

Professor Bauer thinks that India should spend more on other purposes, such as agriculture, roads, and education, rather than on steel mills. If the United States Government, or any other aid-giving body, should agree with him, its appropriate course seems clear. It should tie its aid to those purposes which it thinks India is unduly neglecting.

But that is not at all what Professor Bauer advocates. On the contrary, he thinks that aid to India should be substantially reduced, and that the amount provided should depend on how far India follows the kinds of policies which he favours rather than 'policies designed to socialize or even to sovietize the most populous country of the non-Communist world'.[7]

I consider this a monstrous proposal. The poverty of India, and therefore her need for aid, is beyond question. Moreover India, in contrast to a number of countries, has a large, well-trained, competent, and honest civil service, which can efficiently administer aid. Yet Professor Bauer suggests that the United States should demand, as the price

[7] (Washington D.C., American Enterprise Association, 1959, p. 116).

of her aid, that India should give up the somewhat socialistic policies which she thinks best and should follow instead the types of policies which he believes more suitable.

I happen to agree with Professor Bauer in his general advocacy of more freedom of enterprise, in his dislike of controls, and in some of his criticisms of the details of Indian economic policy, although I think we should bear in mind that the general conditions of life in India, and the character and beliefs of her people, are so different from those of a Western country that we cannot be too dogmatic about the particular forms of 'capitalism' or 'socialism' which are most appropriate. But even if it were sure that the economic growth of India would be speeded up by radical changes in general policy, that would be no justification for the United States refusing aid unless these changes are made.

I do not believe that India is likely to become a police state and to suppress personal freedoms. Should this happen, whether in India or in any other country, I would agree that aid should be refused. Meanwhile, any danger of a movement in this direction is likely to be strengthened rather than weakened by a marked reduction in aid. Economic policies are in quite a different category. We may think that a country has too much government control, or too many state enterprises, or is trying to industrialize too rapidly. We may offer it advice on these lines, but we must recognize that these are controversial questions on which different people hold different views, and that the most suitable measures for any particular country depend on its special circumstances. We may think that a country is making mistakes, but that does not release us from our moral duty to relieve its poverty, nor does it justify us in making aid conditional on its adopting the pattern of economic policy which we happen to favour.

In the past, a good deal of economic aid has disappeared

en route, without achieving the purpose for which it was intended. Some of it has gone into the private pockets of Ministers and others in the recipient countries. Some plant and equipment has rusted away because nobody knew how to assemble it or to use it. Some reports of technical advisers have been ignored because nobody knew what to do with them. Nothing would be gained by reviving old scandals, of which there are plenty. I will mention only one major example. The $2 milliard provided by the Government of the United States to the Government of China during 1945–9 were in effect completely wasted owing to 'the basic maladjustments of the Chinese economy and the malpractices of its administration'[8]

Corruption and waste are not arguments for giving no economic aid at all. They are arguments for making sure that projects are carefully planned; that some are not left incomplete (for example, power stations without transmission lines or dams without irrigation canals) for lack of funds; that plant and equipment are suitable for the country and trained workers are available to use them, and that their products can be marketed; that experts are not provided without the necessary equipment or, conversely, that there is co-ordination of aid provided from different sources; and that, in general, aid does achieve the purposes for which it was provided.

All this implies some kind of effective supervision. It is neither fair to the recipient countries nor to the aid-giving countries that money should be thrown away.

FORMS OF AID

The major choice between forms of aid is between loans and grants. The United States Government is considering

[8] United States. Dept. of State, *United States Relations with China* (Washington, USGPO, 1949), p. 407.

switching over, to a considerable extent, from grants to loans. The nine-nation Development Assistance Group seems to be thinking mainly in terms of loans. A number of underdeveloped countries have expressed their preference for them, although they would of course like them at low rates of interest and with easy terms of repayment, if possible in their own currencies. The assistance provided by the International Development Association will consist largely of loans of this type.

No doubt loans would be more acceptable to the industrial countries, for in so far as they would be repaid later they would be providing 'aid' at little real cost to themselves. But surely the interests of the underdeveloped countries should come first. Most of them are increasing their output and income per head, if at all, at a much slower rate than most of the more advanced countries. Interest and repayment charges would be a heavy burden to them.

This can be illustrated by Brazil, which is not one of the poorest of the underdeveloped countries. Towards the end of 1959 the total foreign-exchange commitments of Brazil for repayment of debts amounted to $2,266 million. (This included loans and credits of $1,456 million for financing special projects and $641 million special balance-of-payments loans.) In 1959 Brazil's export earnings were $1,282 million, and any substantial increase in the near future seems unlikely. The average annual amount required for debt service over the next five years is almost exactly one-fifth of this figure. Will it not obviously be a great burden on Brazil to have to use one-fifth of her export earnings in meeting these foreign-exchange commitments instead of in purchasing imports or building up her foreign-exchange reserves?

To provide a country with aid, more or less continuously, in the form of loans is to saddle it with an ever-mounting burden of debt charges. The Government will have to meet these charges out of its budget. They will therefore impose a growing limitation on its ability to make current developmental expenditures.

The debt charges will also require foreign exchange. Unless the country shows enough restraint in its monetary policy, these growing foreign-exchange commitments are likely to involve it in balance-of-payments crises from time to time. It will be forced to seek desperately for still more loans for 'stabilization' purposes (and such loans will inevitably keep down the sums which it can borrow for development purposes) and probably to place severe restrictions on its imports.

My conclusion, therefore, is that—apart from loans for self-financing projects, such as those provided by the World Bank—the best form of aid is grants and not loans. It is true that in the long run grants will cost the aid-providing countries much more than loans, but this merely reflects the much greater benefits conferred on the recipients.

The chief reason why some underdeveloped countries express a preference for loans is that loans give the industrial countries no excuse for interfering in their political or economic affairs. So long as the payments of interest and repayments of principal are made in full on the due dates, as stipulated in the terms of the loan, the details of how it is spent are no concern of the creditor. The independence of the borrowing country remains inviolate.

This does not apply to grants. A country which makes grants is entitled to make sure that they fulfil their purpose and are not frittered away in corruption and waste. This is the main reason why a number of underdeveloped countries say that they would prefer loans. They fear that grants would give the industrial countries an excuse for interfering in their political and economic affairs.

One possible solution would be for the industrial countries to provide 'soft' loans on easy terms, knowing full well that it was unlikely that their loans would ever be repaid, that when the time came for repayment a borrowing country would seek another and larger loan to cover its commitments. I think it would be a great mistake to pander to 'national pride' in this way. The consequence might well be difficulties and perhaps recriminations, with no assurance that the corruption and mistakes of the past would not be repeated.

The right solution is surely to channel grants through the relevant organizations of the United Nations. An under-developed country could accept the assistance and super-vision of the United Nations in the administration and co-ordination of its grants without any affront to its national pride and dignity. While grants would normally be in money, some might take the form of gifts of surplus agricul-tural commodities, notably from the United States. It is ridiculous that the United States should be embarrassed by large and growing stocks of food while people elsewhere go hungry. The objection raised by countries such as Canada and Australia, that this would interfere with their normal export trade, reflects a very selfish attitude. Canada and Australia are among the wealthiest countries in the world; they can well afford some fall in their export earnings as a contribution (the direct cost of which would be borne not by them but by the United States) to the relief of poverty. For the poorer exporting countries (such as Burma and Thailand, if rice were involved) special arrangements could be made to compensate them for any loss.

CHANNELS OF AID

At present by far the greater part of all economic aid is provided bilaterally, on a Government-to-Government

basis. I believe that it would be better to channel all economic aid through the United Nations. This would make
possible both a distribution of aid more in accordance with
need and effective supervision of its administration in the
recipient countries, which would have no grounds for com-
plaints of 'interference' if the supervision were by the
United Nations.

As Sir William Hayter has put it:[9]

The political end we should now be aiming at is not the earning
of gratitude, or the establishing of political influence in the recipient
country, or defeating opposing ideologies. We should have learnt
by now, and the Russians should learn soon, that these ends are
not achieved by economic aid. Our political end should be the
actual raising of the living standards of Asia and Africa, in the
interests of the people of those countries, but also in the interests
of a stable and peaceful world.

The chief aid-giving countries, however, have not yet
learned these lessons and it is almost certain that the bulk
of economic aid will continue to be provided bilaterally.
Nevertheless it might be possible to expand considerably the
amount of aid provided through the United Nations. The
most effective way to do this would be to set up SUNFED
(Special United Nations Fund for Economic Development).
This proposal was discussed for several years but was not
accepted because the chief industrial countries claimed they
could not afford the contributions required to provide it
even with a capital of $250 million. Now that they are
declaring how important it is to provide a larger flow of
economic aid, they might be prepared to reconsider their
views. The underdeveloped countries themselves were
strongly in favour of SUNFED, and undoubtedly still are.
They welcomed it partly because they would have had some
voice in its affairs; they have no voice in the affairs of an
institution such as the International Development Associa-

[9] 'Aid and Influence', *Observer*, 8 May 1960.

tion, which is an affiliate of the World Bank. They welcomed it also because its aid would have consisted partly of outright grants. Now that IDA has been established (in September 1960) for the purpose of making loans on easy terms, the aid provided by SUNFED should, in my view, consist entirely of grants.

Some industrial countries, notably the United States, probably disliked the proposal for SUNFED partly because the Soviet Union might have taken part in it. I have argued earlier that this attitude is mistaken, and that we should welcome more aid for underdeveloped countries from the Soviet Union. There are signs that this attitude is changing; for example, the United States has accepted the Soviet Union on the Governing Council of the United Nations Special Fund (for financing pre-investment research activities), to which the United States provides 40 per cent. of the member-nations' contributions. Why not? The Soviet Union has no veto and the Soviet bloc has only a small minority of the votes. If SUNFED should be established, its funds should bear some relation to the needs of the underdeveloped countries. A capital of $250 million is ridiculously small. Something of the order of at least $1,000 million each year would be nearer the mark.

Multilateral aid through the United Nations could be extended in other ways also. For example, the Special Fund aims at contributions of $100 million a year from its member-nations (supplemented by appropriate contributions from the recipient countries). The field which it covers[10] is so wide that it could make good use of at least double that amount. Again, the main purpose of IDA is to make loans 'on terms which are more flexible and bear less heavily on the balance of payments than those of conventional

[10] See above, p. 77.

loans'.[11] Presumably IDA loans will be mostly 'soft' loans, repayable in the currency of the borrowing country and on easy terms. There may well be such heavy demands for such loans that after a time the capital of IDA, at present $1,000 million, will need augmenting. Other forms of United Nations aid, such as the expanded technical-assistance programme, are restricted by the limited funds available from contributions by member Governments.

Hence there are various ways in which the industrial countries could, if they wished, contribute more through United Nations channels whilst retaining their own bilateral aid.

It is very important to make sure that aid, whether bilateral or multilateral, is not wasted. The industrial nations, whilst retaining their right to determine to which countries and for what purposes their bilateral aid should be provided, might be prepared to entrust the supervision of its administration to a committee set up for that purpose in each recipient country. They might even be prepared, in order to give no grounds for charges of 'interference', to have no representatives of their own on these committees, provided that the committees included international experts whose competence and integrity were recognized. Such a country committee might consist of the Minister of Planning (or his equivalent) as chairman, one or two other local people, and two or three international experts. The latter might perhaps be nominated by the World Bank, which has a wide knowledge of the experts available in this field.

One task of such a committee would be to see that external aid from different sources was properly co-ordinated, without duplication or overlapping, and that it fitted into the

---

[11] *International Development Association. Articles of Agreement . . . and Accompanying Report of the Executive Directors . . . 26th January 1960* (Cmnd. 965), p. 9. (Art. 1.)

general framework of the country's development plan. No doubt the committee would have before it various offers of external aid. No doubt there would be also a number of gaps, for which it would request external aid from whatever sources it considered most suitable. The committee, and especially the international experts on it, would act as a watchdog for the aid-giving countries and institutions, making sure that their aid was used efficiently and for the purposes for which it was provided. The committee would issue fairly detailed annual reports, and if the international experts wished to express dissenting opinions on any matters they would be entitled to do so.

Regional planning may become of greater importance than at present. The United Nations has its regional Economic Commissions, which serve as a meeting-ground for representatives of different countries, who can discuss their common problems and compare notes on the measures by which particular countries have attempted to deal with them, and on the reasons for the comparative success or failure of such measures. One country might lend another technical experts in a field in which it has made good progress, or might provide training in that field for students from other countries in the region with similar conditions and problems. All this takes place already, but on rather a small scale.

Whether the countries of a region would be willing to agree on regional location of industry, some countries refraining from establishing certain industries if they could import the products from another country in the region more cheaply than they could produce them for themselves, is perhaps doubtful. Economic nationalism, which tends to ignore comparative costs, is very strong in most countries.

The same end might be achieved by regional 'common markets'. Any move towards greater freedom of trade, and greater mobility of capital and labour between countries, is to be welcomed. A number of countries, including some of the newly-independent countries in Africa and elsewhere, are comparatively small and would gain by forming part of a regional group, at any rate for economic purposes. The danger is that a proliferation of 'common markets' may reduce world trade if tariffs and other restrictions on imports from outside countries are increased in order to protect trade within the regional group.

STRINGS OR NO STRINGS?

I recapitulate briefly my views on this subject, and add two or three further points.

Ideally, an aid-giving country should attach no conditions ('strings') to its aid which are designed to increase its political or economic influence in the recipient country or to serve as a weapon against Communism or to expand its trade. The sole purpose should be to promote economic growth and to raise standards of living. Some strings, however, seem desirable in the interests of the recipient countries themselves.

One condition which might be laid down—at least as a general principle—is that the country should maintain the basic human rights and the basic freedoms of the individual. It may be necessary at times (as possibly, for example, in South Vietnam at present) to depart from this principle to some extent in order to cope with threats to internal security from armed bands of terrorists, but repressive measures should not be sanctioned if their purpose is to keep in power a Government which is unpopular with the mass of the people.

If a country clearly suffers from marked and growing overpopulation, aid-giving countries should be entitled to say that they would refuse aid unless the country gave high priority to measures aimed at keeping down the number of births.

International bodies can attach conditions to their aid without being accused or suspected of any motive other than a desire to serve the best interests of the recipient country. The World Bank attaches detailed conditions to its loans; if an applicant country does not accept them, it does not get the loan. The International Monetary Fund is a more suitable source than an industrial country (such as the United States) for providing assistance to a country which has large present and prospective deficits on its balance-of-payments owing to inflating and over-importing. It is fully justified in laying down conditions (as to the monetary and financial policies which the recipient country should follow) designed to prevent a recurrence of these difficulties.[12] In so far as the present constitution of the Fund does not permit it to provide sufficiently large amounts, its constitution should be revised (for example, by permitting it to advance foreign exchange against collateral securities, as I suggested towards the close of Chapter III).

I do not agree, however, that an aid-giving country should refuse or curtail its aid to an underdeveloped country because it disagrees with some aspects of the latter's development plan and economic policies. If it considers, for example, that the development plan includes the establishment or expansion of certain industries which can be profitable only by placing severe restrictions or even prohibitions on competing imports, and will prove a drain on the resources of the country, it can justifiably refuse to assist such industries. But if the country is determined to have them, its economic

[12] There is also a fund (of $60 million) attached to the European Monetary Agreement for assisting members in balance-of-payments difficulties. They are required, as a condition of assistance, to follow the monetary and financial policies prescribed for them.

growth will be further hampered by the cutting-down of external aid. The aid-giving country can earmark its aid for other purposes which it thinks will benefit the recipient country. It can advise the latter to seek aid for industries which (rightly or wrongly) it considers unsuitable, from other sources, such as the Soviet Union, which believes that countries should begin their economic development by establishing industries, especially heavy industries. An aid-giving country has every right to make sure that its aid is not wasted through corruption or incompetence. It can obtain this assurance, without itself 'interfering', through a local committee, including international experts, established for this express purpose.

HOW MUCH AID?

If it is agreed that economic aid is necessary and desirable, the question then arises of how much. On what principles should the annual amount be determined? One method of approach to this question is to estimate how much aid would be required to raise the real incomes per head of under-developed countries by a certain percentage each year. Thus a group of experts reporting to the United Nations estimated that 'a 2 per cent. increase in the per capita national incomes cannot be brought about without an annual capital import well in excess of $10 billion'.[13] That was in 1951; their estimate of $10 billion would be substantially higher today, owing to the rise in prices since 1951.

Mr Hoffman uses the same method of approach.[14] He takes the average income per head of his 'hundred countries'

[13] U.N. Dept. of Economic Affairs, *Measures for the Economic Development of Under-Developed Countries*, Sales No. 1951.II.B2. (N.Y. 1951, p. 79). For a criticism of this report see 'United Nations Primer for Development' by Professor S. H. Frankel in his book *The Economic Impact on Under-developed Societies* (Oxford, Blackwell, 1953), pp. 82–110.

[14] *One Hundred Countries*, pp. 45–47.

at $100 a year and assumes that it is increasing at the average rate of 1 per cent. a year. He estimates that in order to raise this 1 per cent. to 2 per cent. additional economic aid (over and above some $4 billion 'overseas investment' which is being provided already) of about $3 billion a year would be needed.

One reason for the higher estimate of the United Nations Committee is that they believe that 'the most urgent problem of these countries is industrialization'; they therefore provide for 'an annual transfer out of agriculture of 1 per cent. of the total working population into employment other than agriculture' and estimate that this would require a capital of $2,500 for each person absorbed into non-agricultural employment.

The first point to be noted about this type of estimate is that even if the proposed objective were achieved, the gulf between standards of living in the industrial countries (or, more accurately, the richer countries) and the less developed countries would continue to widen.

Incomes in the former are so much higher than in the latter that for them the same percentage increase means a much greater absolute increase. The industrial countries are increasing their own incomes per head by at least 2 per cent. a year; some (for example, France, West Germany, and Italy) by much more. In the United States an increase of 2 per cent. per head is equal to over $40 a year, in the United Kingdom to over $20 a year, in the underdeveloped countries to only $2 to $3 a year.

The second point is that some underdeveloped countries are much poorer than others. If aid were provided solely to relieve poverty, they would need considerably larger amounts per head than the others; their incomes per head should be raised by much more than the average percentage of 2 (or whatever it may be). On the other hand, as Mr

Hoffman says,[15] it is possible that, say, 'ten or fifteen or more key countries will make the most of the opportunities offered, plan and build wisely, attract a disproportionate amount of outside investment, and achieve real breakthroughs towards self-propelling, self-generating economies with enormous increases in living standards'. I think it is optimistic to suppose that 'ten or fifteen or more' countries may do this, on their share of an extra $3 milliard a year. But there may well be an argument for providing a larger proportion of aid, as time goes on, to those countries which use it most fruitfully, rather than to those which are poorest.

The third point is that, in my view, as I have urged earlier, aid is best provided mainly in the form of grants, supplemented by public and private investment. The United Nations Committee and Mr Hoffman equate aid with capital investment. Moreover their estimates (like other estimates of this type) assume a fixed average capital-output ratio. Thus Mr Hoffman assumes an average capital-output ratio of three to one: '$3 billion in capital is needed to yield $1 billion in income'. (The Indian Planning Commission assumes for the Third Five-Year Plan a capital-output ratio of 2·53 to 1.) I have no confidence whatever in the assumption of a fixed capital-output ratio as an instrument of planning; on this point I agree entirely with the criticisms of Professor Bauer.[16]

Personally, therefore, in estimating the amount of economic aid required I would reject any method which attempts to calculate how much would be needed to raise incomes per head in the underdeveloped countries by such-and-such a percentage a year. The fact is that most countries need

[15] *One Hundred Countries*, p. 45.

[16] *United States Aid and Indian Economic Development*, pp. 35–40. Compare also my remarks on the relation between investment and economic growth on pp. 40–41 above.

all they can get, and far more than they are likely to get. The real question is how much the industrial countries can be persuaded to provide.

In this connexion, I should perhaps mention an argument which has been put forward by some industrial countries. They say that it would be unwise for them to provide much, if any, increase in their economic aid, at any rate for some time, since they must first strengthen their own economies. On the same reasoning, a wealthy man might tell his poor relative that in order to provide more adequate help later on he must first plough back his profits to expand his business. Meanwhile, his relative may be starving, or unable to pay for the tools or the training which would enable him to earn a better living. It is true that in order to provide external aid (other than by direct gifts of commodities) a country must develop an export surplus. But this can always be achieved, given the will to achieve it, by suitable monetary and public-finance measures which increase saving relatively to consumption.

Another argument sometimes put forward for restricting the amount of external aid is that a number of under-developed countries have only a limited capacity for absorbing it. It is true that in the past some countries were not able to utilize all the aid available to them. This was because aid was offered to them before they had drawn up their development plans and had arranged to obtain the equipment, and the administrators, engineers, and other skilled personnel required to carry them out.

If mistakes are to be avoided, a public development plan should be carefully drawn up in the light of the resources likely to be available, both locally and from external aid. This takes some considerable time. Although a development plan should be flexible, and subject to revision from time to time owing to changes in relevant circumstances, it requires a great deal of thought and investigation. A number of things may seem urgently needed, but resources are limited, so that priorities must be decided on. A Government should not embark on a project unless it is sure not only that it will serve a useful purpose but also that the resources which it will absorb could not be better used in some alternative way. The technical aspects of each project should be examined; to give just one example, it is futile and wasteful to provide an area with irrigation canals if the water is going to leak through and bring salt to the surface. A project should be properly 'phased'. A large expansion of education, for instance, may require a number of additional schools, but it is useless to build the schools without providing the teachers for them; one of the first measures must be teacher-training.

If a country is prepared to accept outside help, virtually everything it needs for a project could be imported. This happened during the war. For example, the American Army drained a swamp to provide a base in Trinidad. It imported all the equipment it needed, all the skilled workers it needed, the houses (prefabricated) for them to live in, the food for them to eat; it built roads and imported the jeeps and cars, and so forth. This kind of thing could be done almost anywhere. Resources may be limited, but not 'absorptive capacity'.

A somewhat similar device (which was followed, for example, by Burma) is for a country to employ one or more foreign firms of consultants to assist in planning its development and in placing contracts for various projects with other foreign firms, who provide the skilled personnel and any special equipment required. Another possibility is for a country to facilitate direct investment by foreign companies; this may include the establishment of 'joint ventures' in which its Government is a partner.

At the moment, there are a number of newly independent countries, especially in Africa, and some of them have been faced with an outflow of skilled foreign personnel. They need to borrow administrators, experts, and technicians, while their own people are being trained. A major source from which they can borrow is the United Nations, which is taking emergency measures to recruit additional personnel, to expand its present 'pool' of experts, in order to meet their requests.[17]

However, although 'limited absorptive capacity' is a myth, in so far as any number of projects can be carried out with sufficient outside help, it remains true that a country will not 'take off' into self-sustaining economic growth unless it has the will to do so, and the appropriate social conditions (including incentives).

I return to the key question of how much more the industrial countries might be willing to provide in economic aid—as distinct from military aid, export credits, and private capital. A figure which has often been suggested is one per cent. of their national incomes. This would amount to a total of some $10 milliard a year, of which nearly half would come from the United States. It is not a large enough sum to achieve any miracles, but it is about three times the amount provided at present.

I propose, therefore, that the more-developed countries should undertake to provide a minimum of $10 milliard a year for the next ten years for economic aid as defined by the United Nations. This would consist mainly of grants (including grants for technical assistance) and I should hope that a considerable proportion of it would be channelled through the United Nations, including especially SUNFED, which should be established as soon as possible with a guaranteed income of at least $1,000 million a year.

[17] *Economic World*, May 1960.

At present, the general practice is for each country to decide annually how much (if anything) it will contribute to each United Nations organization (such as United Nations Technical Assistance or the United Nations Special Fund) for the coming year. This makes it impossible for these United Nations organizations to plan their expenditure on a firm long-term basis. Contributions would be more valuable if they were promised in advance, at the rate of so much a year, for several years ahead.

The same applies to bilateral economic aid, but here there is a complication. Some countries may make excellent use of their economic aid, so that aid-giving countries might wish to increase the annual amounts provided for them. Other countries, for one reason or another, might not make good use of it and might spend the amounts provided somewhat wastefully, merely for the sake of spending them. Aid-giving countries might therefore reserve the right, in such circumstances, to reduce the annual sums which they had provisionally guaranteed to such countries, and to give the amount of the reduction to the United Nations or to other countries.

The proposed contributions should be increased if prices rise, in order to prevent their real value from falling. Economic aid from the Soviet Union and other Communist countries would be additional to the $10 milliard, and should be welcomed.

It must be remembered that real incomes per head in most industrial countries are rising at the rate of at least 2 per cent. a year. The proposed contributions would not stop this upward trend, but they would make it somewhat flatter.

How would this proposal affect the United Kingdom? This country is already providing over $100 million a year in economic aid (as defined by the United Nations). Assuming that incomes continue to rise it would have to provide about a further $100 million a year. This is equivalent to about an additional 3d. on the standard rate of income-tax. Leaders of the Conservative Party have expressed the view that economic aid is of great importance, and the Labour Party in its policy statement of May 1957 adopted the figure of 1 per cent. of national income as the amount which should be provided.

What the British worker would say is more doubtful. He might say that the burden should be borne by the rich. But nowadays most of the rich have disappeared. In 1958 there were only 195,000 persons in the United Kingdom with gross incomes of over £2,000 a year and their total incomes amounted to only £551 million after tax.[18] The rich are already taxed almost to the limit, if incentives to effort, enterprise, and investment are to be maintained. Again, he might say that the money for aid should be raised by annual internal loans. But this would deprive British industry of some investment (which would tend to raise his earnings) and after a time the cumulative increase in interest charges on the national debt would cost him more in taxation than a policy of pay-as-you-give.

If British economic aid is to be doubled, much of the cost will fall on wage and salary earners. But from the world standpoint, they are 'the rich'; their incomes fall within the highest 10 per cent. of all the personal incomes in the world. The average male manual worker earns over £14 a week, and this is likely to rise year after year. He would be required to pay something under two shillings a week, in one way or another, as his share of the British contribution to underdeveloped countries, where most of the people earn only £1 to £2 a week. It is possible that he might be prepared to make this sacrifice.

[18] Great Britain. Central Statistical Office, *National Income and Expenditure, 1959*, Table, 22.

At the moment of writing, the prospects of a substantial increase in economic aid do not seem very favourable. The United States is worried about the deficit on her balance of payments, and has expressed the view that the countries of Western Europe, now that they have made such a striking economic recovery from the setback of the war, should bear a larger part of the burden of economic aid. France has been more generous in the past, in relation to her national income, than any other country, and is burdened with the cost of the Algerian war. The United Kingdom has special responsibilities to her colonies and to her ex-colonies which have recently attained independence. All these three countries look hopefully to West Germany, which so far has not been very forthcoming.

The whole question is still befogged by misconceptions. There is the misconception that somehow economic aid can be given without real sacrifice—for example, by loans or by stimulating private investment. Private investment can undoubtedly play a valuable part and in some cases loans are appropriate. But I repeat once again that the aid which is of most benefit to recipient countries is aid in the form of outright grants, which do not bear interest and have not to be repaid.

Again, the view still prevails that economic aid is a powerful weapon against Communism or a means of directly promoting exports. The question is still asked: 'What do *we* get out of it?' The answer is that we should expect nothing, not even gratitude. The purpose of economic aid is simply to relieve the poverty of our much less fortunate fellow human-beings and to help them to speed up the economic growth of their economies. Once the needs of the underdeveloped countries are taken as the sole criterion, 1 per cent. of national incomes which are far higher per head than theirs, and growing much faster, should surely be the very least which we are willing to contribute towards a better world.

POSTSCRIPT

More recent data on 'international economic assistance to the less developed countries' (as the United Nations now terms economic aid) are now available in the U.N. document E/3395 of July 1960. This document contains a number of interesting discussions and tables, and includes a survey of economic assistance by Communist countries.

In the year 1958–9 the net total, excluding bilateral aid from Communist countries, was some $3·5 milliard. The proportion provided as loans rather than grants has risen over the last five years from 27 to 37 per cent. Over 90 per cent. of economic aid in 1958–9 was provided bilaterally. The major contributions of bilateral aid were (in millions of dollars): the United States 1,807 (grants 1,132, net loans 675), France 746 (grants 693, net loans 53), and the United Kingdom 207 (grants 136, net loans 71). The contribution of Germany (F.R.) was 76 (grants 5, net loans 71).

It will be seen that the United States substantially increased her contributions in the form of loans. A growing part of American aid has been associated with the disposal of surplus agricultural commodities, either as outright gifts or by sale for local currencies. The proceeds of the latter have gone largely as grants for local economic development or as loans to private enterprises in the purchasing countries.

Preliminary estimates for 1959–60 show a sharp rise in the United Kingdom's contribution, to $324 million, partly in the form of Commonwealth Assistance loans.

Among the recipient countries India showed a large increase in 1958–9. During that year she received $613 million net, including a loan of $284 million from the World Bank.

PRINTED BY
THE CHAPEL RIVER PRESS LTD.
ANDOVER, HANTS